THE BEDFORD SERIES IN HISTORY AND CULTURE

The Confessions
of Nat Turner

WITH RELATED DOCUMENTS

SECOND EDITION

Edited with an Introduction by

Kenneth S. Greenberg

Suffolk University

bedford/st.martin's
Macmillan Learning
Boston | New York

For Bedford/St. Martin's

Vice President, Editorial, Macmillan Learning Humanities: Edwin Hill
Publisher for History: Michael Rosenberg
Senior Executive Editor for History: William J. Lombardo
Director of Development for History: Jane Knetzger
Developmental Editor: Alexandra DeConti
Marketing Manager: Melissa Famiglietti
Production Editor: Lidia MacDonald-Carr
Production Coordinator: Carolyn Quimby
Director of Rights and Permissions: Hilary Newman
Permissions Assistant: Michael McCarty
Permissions Manager: Kalina Ingham
Cover Design: William Boardman
Cover Art: Capture of Nat Turner after the Southampton Insurrection, Etching, 1831 /
    GLASSHOUSE IMAGES / Private Collection / Bridgeman Images
Project Management: Books By Design, Inc.
Composition: Achorn International, Inc.
Printing and Binding: RR Donnelley and Sons

Manufactured in the United States of America.

1   0   9   8   7   6
f   e   d   c   b   a

For information, write: Bedford/St. Martin's, 75 Arlington Street, Boston, MA 02116
    (617-399-4000)

ISBN 978-1-319-06486-0

Acknowledgments

*Acknowledgments and copyrights appear on the same page as the text and art selections they
cover; these acknowledgments and copyrights constitute an extension of the copyright page.*

Foreword

The Bedford Series in History and Culture is designed so that readers can study the past as historians do.

The historian's first task is finding the evidence. Documents, letters, memoirs, interviews, pictures, movies, novels, or poems can provide facts and clues. Then the historian questions and compares the sources. There is more to do than in a courtroom, for hearsay evidence is welcome, and the historian is usually looking for answers beyond act and motive. Different views of an event may be as important as a single verdict. How a story is told may yield as much information as what it says.

Along the way the historian seeks help from other historians and perhaps from specialists in other disciplines. Finally, it is time to write, to decide on an interpretation and how to arrange the evidence for readers.

Each book in this series contains an important historical document or group of documents, each document a witness from the past and open to interpretation in different ways. The documents are combined with some element of historical narrative—an introduction or a biographical essay, for example—that provides students with an analysis of the primary source material and important background information about the world in which it was produced.

Each book in the series focuses on a specific topic within a specific historical period. Each provides a basis for lively thought and discussion about several aspects of the topic and the historian's role. Each is short enough (and inexpensive enough) to be a reasonable one-week assignment in a college course. Whether as classroom or personal reading, each book in the series provides firsthand experience of the challenge—and fun—of discovering, recreating, and interpreting the past.

Lynn Hunt
David W. Blight
Bonnie G. Smith

Preface

The Nat Turner slave rebellion erupted in Southampton County, Virginia, during the early morning hours of August 22, 1831. It was brutally repressed in little more than a single day. At its height, the revolt involved approximately forty active rebels and ultimately led to the death of approximately fifty-five white victims. While we can be reasonably certain of the number and identities of the black rebels who were executed after trials, and we can clearly identify the white victims, there were scores of additional "anonymous" deaths: unrecorded summary executions of "suspected" insurrectionists by infuriated local residents and militiamen.

By some measures, the Nat Turner slave rebellion was a minor event. It never posed a direct threat to the security of the slave regime. The bulk of the killing ended quickly. Nearly all the deaths occurred within the limits of a single county. The rebellion was repressed by a small number of men from local militia units. Although the insurrection was one of the largest slave revolts in the United States, it was quite small compared with many revolts in Latin America and the Caribbean.

And yet the Nat Turner rebellion is a vitally important event for any student of American history. It is less important for what it accomplished immediately in terms of death and destruction than for its longer-lasting consequences, for what it reveals about slavery and the nature of antebellum society, and for what it can tell us about African American traditions of resistance. Careful study of the revolt and its aftermath can tell us much about masters, enslaved people, and relations between them in the antebellum South. Who was Nat Turner? What were his thoughts and motives? Was he part of an African American tradition of slave resistance, or was he unique? What led to the insurrection in Southampton? How did masters and political leaders react to the rebellion? What do these reactions reveal about the attitudes of the ruling group toward slavery and enslaved people? How did blacks react to the rebellion? What were the ultimate results of the revolt? This book includes the documentary evidence that allows students to begin to probe these and many additional related questions.

The central document of this volume, presented in Part Two, is the confession of the enslaved rebel Nat Turner. Shortly after Turner's capture, local lawyer Thomas R. Gray visited him several times in his jail cell, recorded a series of confessions, and quickly published them in pamphlet form. The document is a rich source of information for historians. We have nothing else like it from any other leader of a slave rebellion.

In addition, to help readers reconstruct the insurrection and to enable them to understand the larger context of events that surrounded the *Confessions*, this volume also includes selected newspaper articles, trial transcripts, and excerpts from the diary of Virginia governor John Floyd in Part Three, Related Documents. It also contains portions of Virginia professor and proslavery theorist Thomas R. Dew's "Abolition of Negro Slavery." Dew's essay offers his analysis of the Virginia legislature's debate on the abolition of slavery conducted in the wake of the Turner rebellion. It was the last thorough and open debate about the abolition of slavery undertaken by a key Southern state during the antebellum era. Dew's analysis reveals the logic of a significant strand of proslavery thought and helps us understand Virginia's rejection of the idea that slavery could be abolished. It documents an important conservative response to the Turner insurrection. New to this edition is a substantial excerpt from David Walker's *Appeal to the Coloured Citizens of the World*. This extraordinary condemnation of slavery and call for African American resistance was written in Boston by a free black man just before the Turner rebellion. While we have no evidence that Turner ever read this document, the circulation patterns of Walker's pamphlet in areas of the South near the rebellion, as well as the striking similarities between the thought of Turner and Walker, are worth the serious consideration of all students of the rebellion. Note that I have chosen to retain original spellings and punctuation—often inaccurate by standards of modern usage—in the documents in this volume.

The introductory essay in Part One serves several purposes. Overall, it places *The Confessions of Nat Turner* and the related documents in the larger historical contexts suggested by the best recent scholarship. Up until very recently, historians had written no new monograph about Turner since 1975. Now we have Patrick H. Breen's *The Land Shall Be Deluged in Blood: A New History of the Nat Turner Revolt* and David F. Allmendinger Jr.'s *Nat Turner and the Rising in Southampton County*. The introduction takes this new scholarship fully into account.

It also references Anthony E. Kaye's work on the importance of neigh-borhoods to the community of enslaved people; Mary Kemp Davis's and Stephanie Camp's works on the role of women in resisting enslavement; and Scott French's and Kenneth S. Greenberg's scholarship on Nat Tur-ner in American memory. The introduction also alerts students to the difficulties associated with interpreting the *Confessions* as a historical document. Given the circumstances of its creation and publication, it is a source that needs to be read and analyzed with extreme care.

Finally, the introduction offers students some thoughts on Nat Tur-ner as a figure of continuing historical controversy and importance. As this volume went to press, the first feature film ever produced about Nat Turner won the top prize at the Sundance Film Festival and sold for the largest amount of money ever paid for a Sundance film. Nate Parker wrote, directed, produced, and starred in this film, entitled *The Birth of a Nation*—a title that provocatively echoes the 1915 film that valorized white racism and the Ku Klux Klan. Parker's film captures much of the substance and spirit of the documentary record included in this volume. However, as one would expect from any feature film, it also includes many inventions—some quite plausible and some less plausible. Stu-dents of the rebellion who have seen Nate Parker's film will be able to use the documents in this volume to contrast Turner as he appears in the film and Turner as he appears in the historical record. This diffi-cult task should generate complex and nuanced conclusions and should prove as challenging as any problem ever faced by students of history.

ACKNOWLEDGMENTS

During the preparation of the first edition of this volume in 1996, I accu-mulated a number of intellectual and professional debts. It was a plea-sure to work with the helpful and supportive staff at Bedford Books, especially Chuck Christensen, Niels Aaboe, Louise Townsend, and Tina Samaha. The outside readers for the press, Edward Ayers, David Blight, Catherine Clinton, Eugene Genovese, and Wilma King, were generous in their praise and constructive in their criticism. Several of my colleagues at Suffolk University selflessly read and commented on my introductory essay, including Robert Allison, John Berg, Luckson Ejofodomi, Robert Hannigan, Alex Hurt, Susan Keefe, Sharon Lenzie, Fred Marchant, Joe McCarthy, and Alexandra Todd. Their support, and the support of the Dean of the College, Michael Ronayne, created an ideal scholarly envi-ronment at Suffolk. I have also benefited from conversations with my

Suffolk students about Nat Turner. Suffolk's reference librarians, Jim Coleman, Kathie Maio, and Joe Middleton, were extremely clever and diligent in helping me track down obscure documents.

In preparing this revised edition, I accumulated a number of additional debts. The staff at Bedford/St. Martin's, especially Developmental Editor Lexi DeConti and Senior Executive Editor William Lombardo, proved efficient and helpful. I would also like to thank Publisher Michael Rosenberg, Director of Development Jane Knetzger, Marketing Manager Melissa Famiglietti, Production Editor Lidia MacDonald-Carr, Cover Designer William Boardman, and Production Coordinator Nancy Benjamin of Books By Design. Dean Maria Toyoda and Department Chair Robert Allison created the kind of supportive atmosphere at Suffolk University that makes it a pleasure to produce scholarly work. My Suffolk colleagues James Carroll and Fred Marchant supplied good friendship and intellectual support. I also want to extend special thanks to Richard and Barbara Rosenberg and Walter Weisman for their help in securing a ticket to *The Birth of a Nation* at the Sundance Film Festival. They moved a mountain to accomplish a nearly impossible task. Finally, my family continued to provide the kind of intellectual and emotional support that makes all my work possible. I want especially to thank Jean Guttman, Laura Greenberg-Chao, Dustin Chao, Amy Ward, Arthur Ward, and Lisa Greenberg. Even my grandchildren—Sam, Jonah, Rafa, and Elliott—contributed in ways that would surprise them. Judi Greenberg continues to be my most important critic and supporter.

Kenneth S. Greenberg

Contents

PART ONE

Introduction:
The Confessions of Nat Turner—
Text and Context

NAT TURNER: THE MAN AND THE REBELLION

The Nat Turner slave revolt began with a dinner.[1] The conspirators met in the woods near Cabin Pond in Southampton County, Virginia, on Sunday, August 21, 1831. Hark brought a pig. Henry carried brandy. Soon they were joined by Sam, Nelson, Will, and Jack. Finally, long after the other men had gathered, Nat Turner made his appearance.

Turner's late arrival was no accident. All his life Nat Turner presented himself and was accepted by the black community as a man apart, a man with extraordinary abilities, destined for some special purpose. When Turner was a child of three or four, his mother overheard him describe events that had occurred before his birth. She declared that one day he would be a prophet. Similarly his parents had noted "certain marks" on his head and chest and told him it was a sign that he was "intended for some great purpose." Turner's grandmother, his master, and many others repeatedly remarked that his extraordinary intelligence made him unfit to be a slave. As a young man, Nat Turner simultaneously devoted himself to the mastery of sacred and secular knowledge—demonstrating spontaneously an ability to read, experimenting with the manufacture of paper and gunpowder, and cultivating an austere lifestyle of religious devotion, fasting, and prayer.[2] His unusual manner, talents, and interests set him apart and marked him as a leader in the community.

1

No evidence exists that Nat Turner's life was distinguished by *unusual* brutality from a master. He did not undertake his revolt as an act of revenge against a particular person. Nat Turner's enemy was slavery rather than his master. Slavery's "routine" brutality was divorced from the character of any one slaveowner. Even a simple recounting of Nat Turner's movement from owner to owner during the course of his life suggests the horror of repeated reshuffling of families and communities. No move was over a large distance, but each must have been experienced as a major disruption caused by circumstances beyond his control. Nat Turner was born on October 2, 1800, the property of Benjamin Turner, one of many small farmers in Southampton County, Virginia. In 1809, Nat Turner passed into the hands of Benjamin Turner's son Samuel. On the death of Samuel in 1822, he was sold to another local man, Thomas Moore; when this new master died in 1827, Turner became the property of Moore's nine-year-old son, Putnam. Two years later, Thomas Moore's widow married carriagemaker Joseph Travis. In August 1831, at the time of the dinner at Cabin Pond, Nat Turner was still the legal property of the boy Putnam Moore, but his effective master was Joseph Travis. That is why the first assault of the 1831 rebellion was Nat Turner's glancing hatchet blow to Joseph Travis's head.[3]

Some time during the early 1820s, Nat Turner experienced the first of a series of religious revelations. One day, while praying at his plough, the "Spirit" (the same Spirit that he believed "spoke to the prophets in former days") visited him and repeated one of his favorite scriptural passages: "Seek ye the kingdom of Heaven and all things shall be added unto you."[4] This vision, repeated two years later, set Nat Turner on the course culminating in the Southampton insurrection of 1831.

From his early childhood until his execution by the state of Virginia, Turner had found in his life and in the natural world a series of signs to be interpreted. The comments that he would become a prophet or that he was unfit for slavery, the marks on his head and chest, his ability to read without being taught, and finally the revelation instructing him to seek the kingdom of Heaven—these signs all seemed to point in a single direction: God had commanded him to lead his people in a great battle against slavery. Nat Turner was a "semiotic" rebel—a man moved to action by reading and interpreting the signs of heaven and earth.

Turner's early revelations were followed by others, all pushing him closer and closer to rebellion. He envisioned "white spirits and black spirits engaged in battle, and the sun was darkened"; he discovered "drops of blood on the corn as though it were dew from heaven"; and he "found on the leaves in the woods hieroglyphic characters, and numbers, with the forms of men in different attitudes, portrayed in blood." Finally, the Spirit visited him once again and "said the Serpent was loosened, and Christ had laid down the yoke he had borne for the sins of men, and that [he] should take it on and fight against the Serpent." All these signs Nat Turner interpreted. He now saw himself carrying the burden of Christ and only awaited a clear signal from the heavens before he would begin his work of judgment.

The signal came in the form of a solar eclipse on February 12, 1831. Turner hesitated and delayed action, but another signal came in the guise of a green-tinted sun on August 13. By this time, the meaning of the heavenly signs seemed unmistakable to Turner, and he organized the Sunday dinner at Cabin Pond—a last supper together with the men he trusted.

The rebels struck the first blow before dawn on August 22 (probably around 2:00 a.m.) at Nat Turner's home farm, the Travis residence. Their basic tactic was to kill all white people at every farm they reached—men, women, and children; to move with great speed; and to gather additional recruits as they moved along. By midday, they had killed people at eleven farms and had enlisted approximately forty mounted insurgents.[5] Turner believed they were now strong enough to attack the aptly named county seat of Jerusalem, a tempting symbolic as well as military target. However, a skirmish with the local militia and the discovery of heavily guarded bridges and roads disorganized and demoralized the insurgents. The final assaults by Nat Turner's much-reduced force were repulsed at daybreak of the next morning. The militia quickly captured or killed all the rebels, with the exception of Turner himself. Nat Turner eluded his pursuers more than two months, never leaving the immediate area but changing hiding places several times. He was finally captured on October 30, tried one week later, and executed on November 11.

THE SETTING

The slavery into which Nat Turner was born was a variation of the unfree labor system common in many parts of the world from ancient times until the late nineteenth century. Virginia slavery was part of the larger system of "New World" slavery developed by European colonizers in the sixteenth and seventeenth centuries. It shared two central features of this modern slavery: It was rooted in the needs of agricultural production; and it was racial—enslaved people were black with African origin, and masters were white with origins in western Europe.

Virginia slavery began in the seventeenth century and grew to full maturity under the impetus of exploding European demand for tobacco. Immense wealth and large numbers of enslaved people came into the hands of the great Tidewater planters of the eighteenth century—men who had access to the world market through the Chesapeake Bay and its tributary rivers. Although the relative prosperity of Virginia began to wane after the American Revolution as greater economic opportunities were found in the cotton, rice, and sugar plantation regions further south and west, Virginia remained an important slaveholding state. Its planters learned to make money by diversifying their crops and by selling off their excess enslaved laborers to faster-growing areas of the South, and its central geographic position and articulate leadership ensured it a prominent place in national politics.

By many measures, Southampton County, Virginia, in 1831 was a relatively isolated, economically stagnant backwater area. Located in southeastern Virginia along the North Carolina border, it was far from both the ocean and from a city of any consequence—seventy or eighty miles from Norfolk and Richmond. The county contained several tiny villages with little more than a church or a country store located at road intersections like Bethlehem Crossroads and Cross Keys; its largest town was the county seat, Jerusalem, with a population of approximately 251.[6] While Southampton County was not in serious economic crisis before the Nat Turner revolt, its relative isolation meant that growth lagged significantly behind other parts of the state. In 1800 the assessed value of land in the county ranked fifth; by 1830 it had declined to forty-sixth.[7]

Southampton County in 1831 was a forested landscape, swampy in places, and dotted with relatively small farms. At least one-third of the white families owned no slave property. The vast majority of masters owned fewer than ten enslaved people, with only 13 percent owning twenty or more. A tiny handful of the county's landholders ranked among the aristocrats of the state who owned more than one hundred people.[8] Although the county was not an area of vast plantations, it did contain a substantial enslaved population—one that significantly outnumbered the white population. The census of 1830 reported 6,573 whites and 7,756 enslaved people. Southampton also contained 1,745 free blacks, an unusually high percentage for Virginia. The free black population had skyrocketed in the late eighteenth and early nineteenth centuries as a result of manumissions undertaken by local antislavery Quakers, Baptists, and Methodists. Overall, if we combine the number of enslaved people and free blacks, Southampton County was almost 60 percent black in 1831.[9] The proportion of African Americans may have been even greater in the lower part of the county, which was the scene of the Nat Turner rebellion.

The majority of Southampton farmers engaged in the mixed agriculture typical of other areas of the upper South. They cultivated corn, cotton, potatoes, and peas; they raised cows, hogs, and chickens. Many kept small orchards of apple trees from which they manufactured a popular and potent brandy in their own stills. While much of what they produced was for consumption on the farm or in the local community, the larger farmers shipped their surplus down rivers to more distant markets.[10]

It is important to begin study of the Nat Turner rebellion by understanding these geographic, economic, and demographic features. They help explain several significant aspects of the revolt. For example, it seems clear that one should not look for the causes of the revolt in any unusual economic conditions in the county. It was not a prosperous area, but neither was it in serious decline. Moreover, the relative isolation of Southampton County, its inaccessible swampy areas, along with its heavily African American population, suggests why Nat Turner might have thought he had a chance of success. Finally, study of the demographic and economic landscape of Southampton County enables us to understand what may be the most significant feature of the rebellion: Blacks and whites in Nat Turner's world faced each other every day. This was not a terrain of absentee landowners who ruled anonymous enslaved people. On most farms, including Nat Turner's, masters and the people they owned lived and worked together in small numbers and in close proximity. One recent historian has noted the "neighborhood" as the primary focus of Nat Turner's rebellion.[11] Hence, this would be an "intimate" rebellion. Many of the black and white casualties knew personally the people who killed them.

THE TEXT

The single most important source for our knowledge of the Southampton rebellion is *The Confessions of Nat Turner.* But, as with any historical source, it is a document that must be approached with care and caution. To make good use of it, one must first understand how and why it was produced. Only then is it possible to consider how it both reveals and conceals the nature of the rebellion — the ways it both expands and limits our vision of Nat Turner and his world. It is best to begin by noting that Nat Turner was not the author of *The Confessions of Nat Turner*—at least not in the conventional sense. He did not write the words that appeared on the printed page, and he did not give overall structure to the document. In a sense, the *Confessions* was a joint production—with many of the major decisions in the hands of local lawyer and slaveowner Thomas R. Gray. Any reading of the *Confessions* must begin with some understanding of Gray and his motives.

Thomas R. Gray was not Nat Turner's lawyer, although he had earlier been appointed by the court to defend several other enslaved people charged in the rebellion. Very likely he knew most, if not all, of the whites killed in the revolt. Certainly he was no friend to Nat Turner. Shortly after Turner's capture on October 30, Gray used his influence with the jailer to gain entry to the prisoner's cell. Here, over a period of three days, from November 1 through 3, Gray interviewed Turner. Gray wrote down Turner's words, along with his own notes and questions, and ultimately cross-examined him to determine consistency and to supply missing information. A week later, on November 10 (the day before Turner was to hang), Gray obtained a copyright for the *Confessions* in Washington, D.C. By the end of the month, the *Confessions* was published in Baltimore and achieved wide circulation—with perhaps as many as 40,000 to 50,000 copies sold, including at least two reprintings.[12]

A complex set of motives very likely impelled Gray to produce *The Confessions of Nat Turner*. For one thing, it was a potentially lucrative venture in terms of money and fame. At the time of the Turner rebellion, the thirty-one-year-old Gray was a man in desperate financial need, a man on the edge of failure as a planter. In 1829 he owned twenty-one enslaved people and a farm of eight hundred acres; by 1831 his holdings were reduced to a single slave and three hundred acres. And in the midst of the trials that followed in the wake of the slave rebellion, his father died after cutting him out of his will.[13] Gray must have understood the economic value of the Nat Turner story. He joined the procession of those who hoped to profit by writing about the suffering of others.

However, Gray also thought of himself as performing a public service. As he explains in the introduction to the *Confessions*: "Public curiosity has been on the stretch to understand the origin and progress of this dreadful conspiracy, and the motives which influences its diabolical actors." Gray hoped his pamphlet would satisfy the public clamor for reliable news. In fact, it would accomplish more, for it is clear that Gray had a vision of the rebellion to convey in his publication. Gray's interpretive presence shapes many aspects of Nat Turner's *Confessions*. He sets the stage in his opening note to the public, characterizing Nat Turner and his companions in ways that indicate his hostility. Turner was a " 'great Bandit,' " "a gloomy fanatic," with a "dark, bewildered and overwrought mind," a man who "begged that his life might be spared at his moment of capture"; the slaves engaged in "cruelty and destruction," they were a "fiendish band," "remorseless murderers," men "actuated by . . . hellish purposes."[14] Gray follows the confession itself with his own version of a trial transcript, including a stern condemnation from the court and the dramatic pronouncement that Turner "be hung by the neck until you are dead! dead! dead and may the Lord have mercy upon your soul." He ends with a somber list of the dead whites and a list of the rebels tried for the insurrection.

Gray's touch extends even into the section of the document that he presents as a verbatim transcript of Nat Turner's confession. In addition to Gray's overt editorial comments in parentheses and interjected questions, certain phrases seem unlikely to have been uttered by Turner. Some scholars have doubted that Turner would have described his early religious experiences as an "enthusiasm" for which "I am about to atone at the gallows." In the nineteenth century, religious "enthusiasm" had negative connotations that seem inconsistent with the way Turner thought of his relation to God. Similarly, these same scholars have wondered about the presence of certain stock melodramatic phrases in the document. Would Turner really have described sending Richard Whitehead to an "untimely death"; would he have said "Vain hope" after a white family shut its door; would he tell us that Mrs. Reese's "son awoke, but it was only to sleep the sleep of death?" Did Turner actually portray himself as viewing "the mangled bodies . . . in silent satisfaction," and did he really say that he searched for "more victims to gratify our thirst for blood?"[15] These phrases have the markings of Gray's editorial voice.

Gray's intrusion of certain phrases into Nat Turner's confession is only a small sign that this was not a verbatim transcript. It is also likely that Gray intentionally or inadvertently organized at least portions of Turner's confession so that it confirmed his own interpretation of the rebellion. Historians Henry Irving Tragle and David F. Allmendinger Jr. have both noted that the *Confessions* includes information contained in a letter dated September 17, 1831, and published in the Richmond *Constitutional Whig* on September 26—weeks before Turner had been captured (see Document 7). They both make a strong argument that, although published without attribution, that article was authored by Thomas R. Gray and that he later shaped at least portions of the *Confessions* to conform to his earlier analysis.[16] Other historians, most recently Patrick H. Breen, do not believe that Gray was the author of the letter published in the *Constitutional Whig*.[17] Whether or not Gray actually wrote this letter, it seems likely that he intended the *Confessions* to bolster a position already articulated by other white Southerners—the belief that Nat Turner was insane. The *Confessions* would never have been circulated had it overtly suggested that the rebellion had roots in the nature of slavery rather than in the madness of a single enslaved person. Gray probably thought the *Confessions* showed the causal connection between the maniacal religious fanaticism of one man and the brutality of the rebellion. In fact, Turner's confessions are divided into two causally connected parts—the first beginning with his early life along with his religious experiences and visions, and the second ending with a detailed and bloody description of the deaths of white people in the rebellion. This structure, coupled with Gray's framing remarks, probably made the document palatable to many white Southern readers. While some Southern communities banned the sale of Gray's pamphlet, it was popular enough to be reprinted in Virginia in 1832.

But *The Confessions of Nat Turner* is far more than the work of Thomas R. Gray. It also includes the voice of Nat Turner. We can hear that voice whenever the *Confessions* contains information that Gray would have had no reason to create or distort. When Nat Turner describes early childhood events, when he gives the details of his religious visions, or when he portrays the planning meeting at Cabin Pond—then we hear Nat Turner. The two most recent major studies of the Turner rebellion agree that the bulk of the *Confessions* was in the voice of Nat Turner and accurately portrayed the key events of Turner's life.[18] Also, just as the *Confessions* contains sections in which Gray shapes Turner's voice, there are also moments when Turner shapes Gray's voice. For example, Gray apparently originally intended to portray Turner as a coward. In his introductory remarks, he notes that Turner was captured "without attempting to make the slightest resistance" and that he "begged that his life might be spared." This description is consistent with earlier newspaper reports of the capture. Yet by the end of the *Confessions*, Gray tells us that Turner's lack of resistance at the moment of capture was due to "the decision of his character" rather than to a fear of death. Turner had convinced Gray that his surrender was calculated—that it was a tactical retreat motivated by the hope of escaping at a more opportune moment. Gray's inconsistent presentation of Turner's capture probably indicates that he changed his mind at some point during his writing. Similarly, although Gray portrayed Turner as a "fanatic" on the subject of religion, his conversations convinced him that "on other subjects he possesses an uncommon share of intelligence, with a mind capable of attaining any thing." Turner had convinced Gray, and many other whites who knew him, that he was intelligent and capable.

In addition to sorting out the two voices in *The Confessions of Nat Turner*, interpreters must also be aware of other complications. To fully understand a historical document it is important to pay attention to what it does not say, as well as to what it does say. It is important to consider the silences in a text. In many ways this is the most difficult aspect of interpretation, because silence is infinite and ambiguous. Did Nat Turner convey all his thoughts to Thomas R. Gray? Just a few months earlier his goal had been to kill all white people. He must have hated Gray as much as Gray hated him. Honest and open dialogue across racial lines was unusual in the antebellum South—so why should we expect it in a conversation between an enslaved and imprisoned rebel and a white lawyer?

This is not to suggest that Turner completely fabricated his confessions. We have too much corroborating evidence that makes it impossible to think of the *Confessions* as a work of fiction. Knowing that he would soon die, Turner probably wanted to tell his story to someone, and Thomas R. Gray was the only person at hand. But he was unlikely to have told everything to Gray. He may have edited himself, or he may have forgotten to speak about many matters that he might have recalled in front of a different audience on a different occasion. For example, although Turner briefly mentioned his family and friends in ways that indicate their powerful influence, he did not describe the full texture of his relations with them. We learn that he once baptized himself and a white man, although whites refused to allow them to use the church and "reviled" them during the ceremony. But he tells us very little about this unusual relationship, which crossed racial boundaries. Turner never describes his reaction to the daily horrors of life as an enslaved person. We learn that "Mr. Joseph Travis . . . was to me a kind master," but this judgment seems disconnected from Turner's first act of violent rebellion—a hatchet blow to Travis's head. Turner must have had a great deal more to say about Travis. We never learn what Turner might have done had he successfully captured the county seat of Jerusalem. It is, of course, possible that Nat Turner commented about all these matters and that Thomas R. Gray deleted his remarks; or perhaps Turner gave no thought at all to these issues. But it is far more likely that Turner engaged in a kind of self-censorship in which he kept silent about many of his deepest thoughts and feelings. He put limits on his intimacy with Thomas R. Gray.

One of the most important gaps in the *Confessions* is the absence of Nat Turner's wife. Although she barely appears in any documents of the period, strong evidence indicates that she existed. The author—possibly Thomas R. Gray—of the September 17 letter published in the Richmond *Constitutional Whig* on September 26 noted that "I have in my possession, some papers given up by his [Nat Turner's] wife, under the lash" (see Document 7). Nat Turner's wife has been identified in several other sources as Cherry or Chary, and historian David F. Allmendinger Jr. has been able to uncover several traces of her life in the public records of Southampton County, including the fact that she and Nat Turner likely lived on the same farm for a dozen years and that there is some evidence they had a son together named Riddick.[19]

But why didn't Nat Turner's wife appear in the *Confessions?* Nat Turner mentioned the important influence of his mother, father, and grandmother, but not his wife. Cherry's absence is consistent with two completely contradictory possibilities—and with a broad range of intermediate positions. Perhaps Nat Turner loved her so deeply that he wished to spare her from possible implication in the rebellion, especially after it had collapsed. Cherry Turner might have been executed or murdered had Nat Turner mentioned her with favor in the *Confessions*. Or perhaps Nat Turner failed to mention his wife because she was no longer a significant part of his life. After all, he had cut himself off from worldly pleasures. For years, he had led an ascetic life devoted to carrying out the commands of God. Nat Turner likened himself to Christ. He had assumed a mission of far greater importance to him than maintaining a close relation with his wife. In other words, Cherry's absence in the *Confessions* could mean that she was at the center or at the periphery of Nat Turner's thought—or some place in between.

The absence of Nat Turner's wife in the *Confessions* reflects the larger absence of African American women in the rebellion. It is easy for a modern reader to miss the heavily male nature of the rebellion, as no contemporary source bothers to mention it. It is part of the "background" of the revolt, which is so central and expected that it is not worthy of special note. But modern readers should be alert to this kind of silence in historical texts. The Nat Turner slave rebellion was initiated and carried out largely by African American men. Only one woman, Lucy Barrow, was arrested and convicted. Her crime was attempting to prevent her mistress from escaping. No black woman directly killed a white person during the rebellion. It is difficult to assess the significance of this fact.

Certainly it is an illustration of the more general gender pattern of resistance by enslaved people. With some notable exceptions, women tended to resist slavery in ways that did not involve violent confrontations or running away.[20] To focus on the gender of the rebels is to become aware of the question of whether black women wholeheartedly supported the rebellion. Did they feel alienated by this insurrection, which destroyed their community as well as their masters? The documentation associated with the Nat Turner rebellion contains bits and pieces of evidence on all sides of this question.[21]

Readers of the *Confessions* must also be aware that the document contains some information that we believe to be inaccurate because it differs from information contained in more reliable sources. Some of these inaccuracies seem inadvertent and relatively insignificant. For example, the appended list of enslaved people tried in the aftermath of the revolt is not fully consistent with the official trial records of the revolt. Also, the list of white victims may not include a few names. More significant are the distortions that seem intended by Gray, distortions designed to enhance his own role, to support the reader's sense of the authenticity of the document, or to heighten the drama of the events. For example, at one point, Gray seems to suggest that the *Confessions* was read to Nat Turner as part of the trial and that Turner acknowledged its accuracy. But the official trial transcript makes no mention of a reading of the Gray confessions in the courtroom and instead refers to a pretrial statement taken by two of the justices (see Document 11). Allmendinger has argued that this apparent discrepancy was not a discrepancy at all. He contends that, if we pay careful attention to the actual words, Gray never really claimed that the *Confessions* was read in court.[22] In any case, it seems clear that the official record of the trial does not mention Gray, but his own version implies that he played a prominent role.

SLAVE REBELLIONS AND RESISTANCE

One way of assessing the meaning and significance of the Nat Turner rebellion is to place it in the context of other rebellions and acts of resistance. This is not a simple matter. As with all issues involving context, the student of Nat Turner has a variety of choices—choices of great consequence that can only be made with reference to larger issues of evidence, purpose, theory, and morality. Such choices should be made with extreme care. To select a context is to magnify or diminish an event or person; to select a context is to determine whether Nat Turner was isolated and inconsequential, whether he was part of a social movement that transformed a society, or whether he had some other significance.

In determining an appropriate framework for understanding the Nat Turner rebellion, one should be aware of the possibilities suggested by other historians. These possibilities do not exhaust all ways of thinking about the revolt, but merely describe the ways of thinking that made sense to some people in the past. Consider the question of the size of the rebellion. The Nat Turner insurrection was among the largest slave rebellions in U.S. history. It is possible to make this claim with some certainty even though we do not have, and may never be able to compile, a complete inventory of American slave revolts. Many rebellions are probably lost to historical memory. Masters generally feared that discussion of insurrections would create unnecessary anxiety among whites or would inspire blacks to additional acts of resistance. Hence some revolts were suppressed without producing a significant trail of documents.[23]

However, the largest rebellions, such as Nat Turner's, have long been known to historians. The larger the revolt, the more likely that it has appeared in the historical record. Colonial New York experienced one major rebellion in 1712 involving two dozen rebels. A 1739 revolt in Stono, South Carolina, involved sixty to one hundred insurgents and resulted in the deaths of approximately twenty-five whites and thirty-five blacks.[24] In addition to the Nat Turner insurrection, three other major conspiracies or revolts occurred in the nineteenth century: Gabriel Prosser's 1800 conspiracy in Richmond, Virginia, with twenty-seven executions; a large but less well known rebellion in southern Louisiana in 1811, probably involving two hundred to five hundred rebels; and the Denmark Vesey conspiracy in Charleston, South Carolina, in 1822, ending in thirty-five executions.[25] Clearly, Nat Turner's revolt ranks high in this group of the largest U.S. rebellions.

Another way to think about the size of the Nat Turner revolt is to place it in a comparative framework with the slave and peasant revolts of places such as Latin America, the Caribbean, and Russia. In this context, the Nat Turner rebellion, along with all U.S. rebellions, becomes greatly diminished in size and revolutionary significance. Consider the comparison with Jamaica, where frequent slave revolts averaged four hundred participants and laid the foundation for a powerful revolutionary tradition by the nineteenth century. After 1731, the Guianas in South America experienced a major revolt every decade; ten thousand to twenty thousand slaves were involved in the 1823 Demerara rebellion. Brazilian rebellions often included many hundreds or even thousands of participants. Communities of tens of thousands of escaped enslaved people sometimes waged guerrilla war for many years. Russian serf rebellions of the seventeenth and eighteenth centuries lasted from nine to fifteen months, involved hundreds of thousands or even millions of participants, and spread over much of the country.[26]

Another possible context for the Nat Turner rebellion is the general framework of acts of resistance. In this context, all rebellions of enslaved people become unusual, ephemeral events. The typical form of resistance to slavery in the United States was not large-scale collective rebellion, but acts of individual or small-group subversion. African Americans ran away — either for a short time or to freedom or quasi-freedom outside the South. They lied, verbally challenged masters, stole food and other supplies, broke tools, feigned illness, slowed the pace of work, beat their masters or killed them with weapons or by poisoning, and burned buildings. Nat Turner's rebellion may have been noteworthy, but it was only a minor part of the larger story of black resistance to slavery. Only forty enslaved people followed Nat Turner, but vast numbers of others resisted in these less spectacular ways.

Some historians have interpreted African American culture itself — distinct forms of religion, music, dance, family structure, or folk tales — as another part of the resistance effort. In this view, any attempt to carve out traditions and practices beyond the reach of white domination can be understood as an act of rebellion. A slave song may be seen as equally or perhaps even more potent than an axe in the larger battle against mastery and control. This approach merges Nat Turner in a broad and deep tradition of African American resistance.[27]

One can also think of Nat Turner as unique — a man who was not part of a social movement or of a tradition of rebellion and resistance. This was the position adopted by Thomas R. Gray when he portrayed Turner as a madman, a fanatic suffering from religious delusions. But this approach need not be associated with a negative view of Turner. Turner's unique qualities can also be praised. Certainly Nat Turner saw himself as different from other people — as chosen by Christ to liberate his people. He would have disagreed with all historical accounts that subsumed him into the stream of a particular culture or social movement. Similarly, William Styron's controversial 1967 Pulitzer Prize–winning novel, like many biographical accounts, also shifts focus away from larger historical continuities toward the unique qualities of the man.[28] Historians disagree about whether Styron's portrait dignified or degraded Nat Turner, but there can be no doubt that the novel depicted an individual rather than a movement.

Finally, it is possible to portray Nat Turner as part of an African American religious tradition of resistance. Any reader of the *Confessions* can see that a religious vision lies at the heart of Nat Turner's view of the world. And his community acknowledged him as a religious leader. Although he was not a formally ordained minister, he was a well-respected lay preacher among his people. Yet if we read the *Confessions* in isolation, it is not clear that Nat Turner was linked to a larger African American religious tradition. He cites no precedent and discusses no connections. He denies conspiratorial or inspirational contact with blacks outside Southampton County; he makes no mention of David Walker's 1829 *Appeal* pamphlet, a religiously inspired call to arms from a Boston African American leader (see Document 15); and he explicitly rejects the African religious tradition of what he calls "conjuring and such like tricks."[29]

However, several historians have suggested that Turner was connected to a larger African American religious community in ways he might not have understood. One has argued that Nat Turner did not have to read what David Walker wrote in order to be linked to him. Both shared an African American religious vision; or, as Vincent Harding has put it, "the God of Walker's *Appeal* had always been in Southampton." Both Turner and Walker believed that their attack on slavery was a "holy crusade" and that "black resistance to slavery was sacred obedience to God."[30]

Others have noted that the sacred dimension so central to the Nat Turner revolt appeared in many other slave rebellions. Denmark Vesey, for example, gathered large numbers of recruits from the African Methodist Episcopal church in Charleston, used its meetings for organization and communication, and repeatedly cited the Bible in his attacks on slavery. One of his chief lieutenants was Jack Pritchard, known as "Gullah Jack," an Angolan conjurer who, among other things, promised invulnerability to recruits who held crab claws in their mouths.[31] While the details of Turner's messianic religious inspiration certainly differed from Vesey's, both men rooted their rebellions in a broader African Christian tradition. Moreover, while Turner explicitly rejected the African conjure activities of men like Gullah Jack, his own religious practices still included elements from a non-Christian African religious past: the markings on his head and breast, which signaled selection for a special purpose; his special relation to "Spirit," which communicated with him and which he tried to serve; and his sense of magical invulnerability—a sense associated with religious leaders in Africa and that appeared in many African American slave rebellions.[32]

In attempting to select from this group of alternatives the best context for the Nat Turner rebellion, one should keep in mind a central point. It is not possible to resolve the question of context by maintaining that all the choices are of equal value. This position is a temptation and may, at first, seem attractive and plausible. At the level of factual accuracy, the contexts do not seem to be mutually exclusive. Careful investigation of the documented historical record seems to show that the Nat Turner rebellion was among the largest U.S. slave rebellions, was small and insignificant by international standards, was unique in many ways, was an unusual form of slave resistance, and was part of an African American religious tradition of resistance.

But at a deeper level, many of the contexts are incompatible because they imply different visions of the purposes of historical inquiry, different conceptions of the nature of social and political order in a slave society, different definitions of what constitutes real change in the world, or different notions of how that change can be accomplished. For example, historian Eugene Genovese placed the Nat Turner revolt in an international comparative context as part of his larger interpretation of the distinct paternalistic nature of Southern slavery: a system in which close personal contact between masters and enslaved people established the nature and limits of resistance. In such a world, it was difficult to produce rebellions with genuine revolutionary potential, with the complex ideology and level of organization necessary to overthrow the old social order.[33]

On the other hand, historian Vincent Harding placed a heroic Nat Turner in a wide and deep river of black resistance, a river that meandered across the centuries of African American history. Nat Turner is a part of Harding's larger inspirational tale "of the harrowing and terrifying beauty of my people's pilgrimage in this strangely promised land."[34] We can admire the work of both Genovese and Harding. We can see that they have virtually no disagreements about the major "facts" of the Nat Turner slave rebellion. But in the end, we cannot simultaneously believe both of them because they have different ideas about the purposes of their inquiry, about the nature of slavery, and about the significance of resistance.

THE AFTERMATH OF THE REBELLION

Virginia whites initially responded to news of the rebellion with a mobilization effort far beyond what was necessary for military victory. Sketchy and incomplete news reports left neighboring communities uncertain about the size of the threat, and their first reactions demonstrated more than a hint of panic. Governor John Floyd heard about the rebellion early Tuesday morning, August 23, long after the local Southampton militia first successfully confronted the insurgents. Floyd ordered militia north of Richmond to ready themselves for action, appointed General Richard Eppes commander of operations in Southampton County, and immediately dispatched militia units from Richmond, Norfolk, and Portsmouth. On his own initiative (and much to the subsequent annoyance of many Virginians who prided themselves on their own ability to control the enslaved population), the mayor of Norfolk asked for the help of federal army and navy units stationed at Fortress Monroe. They were joined by militia and vigilante groups from Isle of Wight, Sussex, and Surry counties, along with units from nearby Murfreesboro, North Carolina. One historian has estimated that at the very moment the Southampton militia had repressed the approximately forty active rebels of the insurrection, nearly three thousand troops began to converge on the county.[35]

While General Eppes quickly sent most of these troops home, the initial size of the mobilization effort offers a good indication of the panic that quickly spread among white Southerners. It was a panic that translated into rumors of the spread of rebellion to nearby communities, into the mobilization of all neighboring militias, into a flood of requests to the governor for weapons, and into a massive effort to root out potential rebels. The brutality of this repressive reaction is easy to overlook. The sources reveal a great deal more about the brutality of the insurgents than of the people who fought them. Violence on the part of the enslaved people is precisely what a slave revolt is all about. A rebellion directed indiscriminately against men, women, and children and fought largely with swords, axes, and farm implements might be expected to produce horrible scenes of cruelty and devastation. Governor Floyd best summarized the images generated by reports from the scene: "Through out this affair the most appalling accounts have been given of the conduct of the negroes, the most inhuman butcheries the mind can conceive of, men, women, and infants, their heads chopped off, their bowels ripped out, ears, noses, hands, and legs cut off, no instance of mercy shown."[36]

But blacks did not have a monopoly on decapitation and other forms of mutilation. One group of whites cut off the head of rebel Henry Porter. It ended up in the hands of a militia surgeon who reportedly carried it with him around the county. The cavalry company from Murfreesboro may have decapitated as many as fifteen suspected rebels and placed the heads on poles for display. One head was posted at the intersection of Barrow Road and Jerusalem Highway—a crossing that then became known as Blackhead Sign Post. We may never know the exact number of summary executions that followed in the wake of the rebellion. Earlier estimates had placed the number at 120 or higher. However, one recent study concluded that the number of blacks killed in the wake of the rebellion has hitherto generally been exaggerated and that the number killed was closer to twenty-four—still a shocking number of people murdered without any formal judicial proceeding.[37]

Even the body of Nat Turner suffered mutilation. One report suggests that just before he was to hang on November 11, "General Nat sold his body for dissection, and spent the money in ginger cakes" (see Document 9). This report was probably only half true. It is unlikely anyone would have given Nat Turner money in exchange for the right to dissect his body. No one ever paid him for the use of his body when he was alive; why would they do so at the moment of his death? But there is strong evidence that his body was dissected. Purported Nat Turner body parts have appeared in several locations since the rebellion ended, including within Southampton County. For example, writing in 1900, local resident and historian William Sidney Drewry concluded that "Nat Turner's body was delivered to the doctors, who skinned it and made grease of the flesh. His skeleton was for many years in the possession of Dr. Massenberg, but has since been misplaced." Moreover, according to Drewry, "There are many citizens still living who have seen Nat's skull. It was very peculiarly shaped, resembling the head of a sheep, and at least three-quarters of an inch thick. Mr. R. S. Barham's father owned a money purse made of his hide."[38] Apparently unaware of the bizarre mixture of horror and irony in their actions, Southampton whites consumed the body and the blood of the black rebel who likened himself to Christ.

Yet there is more to the story of the brutality of the revolt and its aftermath. It was not a simple tale of unrestrained slaughter on all sides. First, consider the insurgents. They did, after all, bypass several houses. One of the conspirators later reportedly confessed that "Capt Nat in passing a house where some very poor people lived said he would not kill them because they thought no better of themselves then they did of the Negroes." The rebels also showed other signs of calculation and restraint. They never burned a building, raped a woman, engaged in an act of torture, or undertook the wholesale looting of valuables. Nat Turner seems to have thought of the slaughter as a temporary tactic. One witness summarized Turner's position shortly after his capture: ". . . indiscriminate massacre was not their intention after they obtained [a] foothold, and was resorted to in the first instance to strike terror and alarm. Women and children would afterwards have been spared, and men too who ceased to resist." Not only was indiscriminate slaughter a plausible tactic under the circumstances, it was consistent with the style of warfare Nat Turner must have read about in the Bible. One can wonder, along with historian Stephen B. Oates, whether Turner had been influenced by the prophet Ezekiel who spoke for Jehovah against the sinners in the Jerusalem of an earlier era. Ezekiel advised his followers to spare only those who remained true to their God, but for those who had broken faith, to "Slay utterly old and young, both maids, and little children, and women. . . ."[39]

Similarly, massacre was not the only white reaction to the rebellion. Many whites were horrified by the wholesale slaughter meted out in the repression of the Nat Turner rebellion. A mixture of motives moved political and military leaders to shift the confrontation quickly from indiscriminate killing in the field to the more careful courtroom dispensation of death. It seemed inhumane to kill people without due process of law; it made Virginia look barbaric in the eyes of the rest of the world; and it destroyed the slave property of masters without the monetary compensation forthcoming when death was dispensed by a legal proceeding. Hence, both Governor John Floyd and some local military commanders took quick action to control the atrocities. One officer threatened the punishment of white transgressors by "the rigors of the articles of war." The governor and commanding General Eppes carefully deployed troops to guard accused rebels and to ensure orderly trials.[40] Nat Turner himself survived a walk through Southampton County and a brief stay in the county jail after his capture.

The trials were far from models of due process, but they did show some concern for the idea of the rule of law. Although some trials took place in neighboring counties, most were held before a group of five magistrates in the Court of Oyer and Terminer at the Southampton County Courthouse. Antebellum Virginia courts of oyer and terminer were a continuation of the county court system of the colonial period. They consisted of justices of the peace appointed by the governor and council, and they had local powers that extended to capital cases involving enslaved people. By any reasonable standards of justice, these were not "fair" proceedings. Rarely have trials been conducted in a jurisdiction so hostile to a group of defendants. And they were completed at a rate that barely distinguished them from summary proceedings—nearly fifty people were tried within a three-week period beginning a little more than a week after the start of the insurrection. While every enslaved person had a court-appointed lawyer, none had the time to put forward a thorough defense.[41]

Yet these trials had other elements. The Court of Oyer and Terminer declined to pass sentence on five free blacks because it did not have jurisdiction over free people in capital cases. One free black defendant was discharged, and the other four were bound over for trial in another court. Eventually three were released, and one was tried and hanged. The justices delayed trials when witnesses were not present. Thirteen trials ended in verdicts of "not guilty" or with a dismissal of the charges. One case was dismissed because of a technical problem with the charge: an enslaved person could not be accused of treason. In several cases— when the defendent sentenced to death was young (sometimes aged fourteen or fifteen) and/or there was evidence that participation in the revolt had been coerced, or the level of participation and proof seemed minimal—the court recommended a commuted sentence and transportation out of the state (see Document 10). Governor Floyd invariably followed the recommendations. Transportation out of the state was a brutal punishment involving permanent separation from family and friends, but the white authorities saw it as a merciful alternative to execution. In the end, thirty people were sentenced to death for participation in the rebellion; only nineteen died on the gallows.[42]

It is important when studying the Nat Turner rebellion to recognize white Virginians' efforts at restraint, the concern for "justice," and the instances of "mercy" at these trials. The goal of such recognition is not to praise masters for humanitarianism and decency. That would miss the point. Rather, the goal is to understand how "mercy" strengthened a slave society. Masters liked to think of themselves as caring and humane in dealing with their slaves. The brutality generated by the initial reaction to the rebellion exposed the ugly force and violence that lay behind the power of the ruling group. The trials should be seen as an attempt to recover from that exposure. Masters were most powerful and most dangerous not when they cut off heads, but when they commuted the death sentences of fifteen-year-old children; not when their power was displayed in its most brutal form, but when their "decency" was displayed in its most benevolent form.

The white Virginians' reaction to the revolt also extended in other directions. One focus was the free black population. It was targeted not simply because some free blacks were thought to have participated in the rebellion. Many whites had long feared the influence of free blacks on slavery. Their mere presence seemed to encourage enslaved people to dream of the possibility of freedom. Hence they were special targets of persecution in the wake of the Nat Turner rebellion. Many fled the county. Perhaps three hundred, or approximately one-fifth the free black population of Southampton, accepted transportation to Liberia offered by the American

Colonization Society. Those who remained had to live under a tightened set of controls, including the elimination of the right to trial by jury.[43]

White Virginians also identified other targets in the wake of the rebellion. Governor Floyd voiced the concerns of many when he wrote fellow governor James Hamilton Jr. of South Carolina with a description of the process by which the "spirit of insubordination" had crept into the state (see Document 13). First came "Yankee peddlers and traders" who helped spread a type of Christianity that undermined slavery. They were followed by Northern preachers who joined with Southern women to teach slaves to read and to write. Their purpose, according to Floyd, may have been an innocent desire to provide blacks access to the Scriptures, but the ultimate results damaged the social order. Finally, "large assemblages of negroes were suffered to take place for religious purposes," assemblages that listened attentively as subversive pamphlets were read aloud by black preachers. In this way, Floyd believed, the incendiary ideas of Northern abolitionists—people like David Walker (see Document 15) or William Lloyd Garrison—spread among the black population of the South. Hence abolitionists were deemed the remote causes of the rebellion, while black preachers were their ultimate agents. In fact, Floyd at one point believed that "every black preacher in the whole country east of the Blue Ridge was in the secret [of the Turner rebellion], that the plans as published by those Northern presses were adopted and acted upon by them."[44]

Not surprisingly, African American preachers and religious practices were a special target of white repression in the wake of the insurrection. Virginia passed laws prohibiting all blacks from preaching or conducting religious meetings. Enslaved people could only attend night religious meetings with their "white families," and they could receive religious instruction only from their masters. For white Virginians, Nat Turner personified the threat of an independent African American religion, and in the wake of the rebellion, they moved to destroy that religion. They failed, of course, but for a while they made a concerted effort.[45]

THE VIRGINIA DEBATE OVER EMANCIPATION

One of the most important consequences of the Nat Turner rebellion was the debate over the future of slavery that occurred in the Virginia legislature in January 1832. It seems that for many white Virginians, the Nat Turner rebellion did not simply mean that new repressive measures had to be taken against the black population; it meant that slavery should be eliminated from the state. The roots of this debate lay in long simmering tensions between the eastern (where the enslaved population was concentrated) and western sections of Virginia over issues like apportionment in the state legislature. In the shadow of the Turner insurrection, the dispute once again bubbled to the surface on December 14, 1831, when a Quaker petition advocating the abolition of slavery was introduced in the legislature. After a short and sharp debate, the legislature voted to refer the petition to a special committee dealing with all slavery-related issues in the aftermath of the Turner rebellion. But the question of emancipation could not so easily be pushed to the side. On January 11, 1832, Thomas Jefferson Randolph, the forty-year-old grandson of Thomas Jefferson, electrified the state with his proposal for a referendum on the issue of ending slavery in Virginia.

Randolph's proposal reflected the combined influence of the Nat Turner rebellion and that of the moderate "antislavery" Virginians of an earlier generation—men like Thomas Jefferson, George Mason, John Randolph, and St. George Tucker. The ideas of these earlier antislavery Virginians were responsible for the mild and cautious tone of Randolph's plan. Nat Turner's revolt supplied the fear and sense of urgency that emboldened Randolph to act; it also gave impetus to the potent anti-black content of the proposal. Thomas Jefferson Randolph proposed *post-nati* emancipation—that all slaves born on or after July 4, 1840, should become the property of the state (men at twenty-one and women at eighteen). After reaching those ages, they could be hired out in order to raise money to pay for their ultimate transportation out of state. The plan was gradualist. No slave could be emancipated until 1858. In fact, no slave *need* be emancipated at all. Before their property reached the designated age, any master had the right to sell a slave to another state; and they had every incentive to do so rather than wait for confiscation. The plan was also anti-black. No freed person would be allowed to remain in Virginia. Those who were not sold out of state before emancipation would be transported.[46] Under the Randolph proposal, the "Day of Jubilee" in Virginia would be celebrated by whites who had rid themselves simultaneously of slavery and blacks. In an echo of the Turner rebellion trials, the entire enslaved population would be shown the "mercy" of a variation of the commuted sentence, including transportation beyond state boundaries.

There is a deep paradox at the heart of the Randolph proposal for emancipation. In one sense, if it had succeeded it would have marked the ultimate triumph of Nat Turner. His dinner at Cabin Pond would be seen as initiating a chain of events that resulted in the elimination of slavery from Virginia. Yet in another way, the triumph of Randolph's proposal would have signified the ultimate defeat of Nat Turner. Slavery would have ended because racism had triumphed. In a perversion of the imagery that inspired Turner, a glowing white sun would be seen to have emerged in the aftermath of a brief eclipse. Slavery would have ended in Virginia while no African American experienced true emancipation.

The Virginia debate over emancipation included a range of positions and complicated legislative maneuvering. In the end, the legislators rejected Randolph's proposal and all its variations. They refused to pass any law moving the state toward abolition. They could agree that Virginia should move immediately to colonize free blacks and manumitted slaves, to ship them to Africa. They could even agree that eventual elimination of slavery from Virginia was a desirable goal. But they would take no action toward implementing that goal.

Within a year, the conservative reasoning that came to prevail during the Virginia debates achieved wide circulation in an essay written by a young College of William and Mary professor of political law, Thomas Roderick Dew (see Document 14). Dew's essay, "Abolition of Negro Slavery," first appeared in the September 1832 issue of the *American Quarterly Review* and was quickly republished in expanded pamphlet form as "Review of the Debate in the Virginia Legislature of 1831–1832." Later, in 1852, it was enshrined as a classic work in the proslavery argument when it was included in the compendium *The Pro-Slavery Argument as Maintained by the Most Distinguished Writers of the Southern States*.[47]

Dew's summary and analysis of the debate included several key elements. Part of the essay, relatively insignificant in the first version but expanded in later editions, was a defense of the morality of slavery noting slavery's legitimate origins, its long history, and its prominent role in the Bible. But the heart of Dew's argument in 1832 focused on the impracticality of all proposals to eliminate slavery. For example, he argued that to emancipate enslaved people born on or after July 4, 1840, would create an enraged and potentially rebellious group born before that date. Also, all plans to compensate masters or to pay for the transport of freed people to Africa would require amounts of money well beyond the resources of Virginia. Any large-scale attempt to colonize blacks in Africa would be doomed to failure for powerful economic and social reasons. And because slavery provided the central economic support to a society committed to the liberty and equality of all white people, its elimination would threaten the freedom so dear to the hearts of white Virginians.

Some historians have labeled Thomas Roderick Dew's essay, along with the events surrounding the Nat Turner rebellion, a momentous turning point in the history of the South.[48] They have interpreted the document as evidence of a great conservative reaction, ushering in a period when white Southerners moved away from the abstract antislavery principles of the Revolution, turned inward, instituted more repressive measures toward the enslaved population, and closed themselves off from the rest of the world. Actually, the Nat Turner insurrection and its aftermath should not be seen as discontinuous with the Southern past. First, repressive measures against enslaved people occurred both *before* and *after* 1831. Nat Turner, after all, was only one man in a long line of other real and imagined rebels. Second, while the Virginia legislature would never again so openly debate the issue of slavery, they would continue to have veiled discussions focusing on how to count enslaved people in matters of legislative apportionment and related issues of representation. And finally, Thomas Roderick Dew and many Virginia legislators still adhered to the dream that one day slavery would be eliminated from the state. Dew, for example, still looked forward to a day when emancipation could come naturally through internal improvements and economic changes that would turn Virginia away from slave-based plantation agriculture. Overall, then, the Nat Turner insurrection and its aftermath should be seen as part of the continuous stream of developments making up the history of the American South.

RETELLING THE STORY

Frequently, retelling a story involves a kind of violation. This is not to condemn the act of retelling, but to describe one easily forgotten part of its nature. The act of recounting, whether personal or historical, often involves transforming the people or events of the past into objects we can use in the present. It does not matter whether we praise or vilify the dead — the full complexity of their lives usually gets lost as we remember them for purposes and in contexts that they cannot share. Those who reconstruct the past are grave robbers. Some treat the corpse with respect, while others mutilate it. Either way, we all rob graves.

Even while Nat Turner lived, he was transformed from a complex whole person into a powerful symbol. In the minds of many white Southerners, Turner was the living embodiment of their worst nightmare: an uncompromising and crazed rebel, a man who had been well treated by masters yet paid them back with death, a savage and merciless baby killer. It was a portrait that lingered among white Southerners long after Turner was executed.

Ironically, many Northern abolitionists shared this image of Turner. William Lloyd Garrison, for example, deplored Nat Turner's violence. His newspaper, *The Liberator*, responded to the rebellion by noting that "we are horror-struck at the late tidings" (see Document 4). While Garrison disagreed with Southern whites who saw Turner as insane, he never praised Turner as a man to be emulated and admired. Although he believed that slavery was the real cause of the atrocity of the rebellion, he still saw it as an atrocity. For Garrison, Nat Turner was the leading edge of the terror that would come on a grander scale if slavery was not abolished. The African American minister Henry Highland Garnet thought of Nat Turner in a similar way. At an 1842 Massachusetts Liberty party convention, Garnet evoked the horror of the Turner insurrection and noted that only enslaved peoples' faith in the ultimate triumph of abolitionism held back "those heaving fires that formerly burst forth like the lava of a burning volcano, upon the inhabitants of Southampton and elsewhere."[49]

While Southern whites and some Northern abolitionists turned Nat Turner into an embodied nightmare, some Virginia enslaved people transformed him into a "trickster" hero. Trickster tales had long been an important part of the folk traditions of African and African American culture. They most frequently assumed the form of animal stories in which a weak creature (a hare, tortoise, or spider in many African stories, and very commonly Brer Rabbit in the United States) used clever tricks to gain an advantage over powerful creatures. While these stories contained the complexity and multiple meanings characteristic of any rich folk tradition, part of their meaning for African Americans involved the mockery of masters tricked by the clever people they owned. In fact, one entire strand of these tales moved away from the animal focus and included the exploits of an enslaved person named John and his master.[50]

In an 1861 *Atlantic Monthly* article on the Southampton insurrection, abolitionist and reformer Thomas Wentworth Higginson included two Nat Turner trickster stories that he believed circulated among the enslaved people of Virginia. In one, Turner was caught in the act of looking at a county map posted on a barn door while he held "lime and lamp black in hand." He tricked his captor with the claim that he was "planning what to do, if he were blind" or that he was "studying how to get to Mr. Francis's house." Similarly, when Turner knew that two poor whites, Mr. Jones and Mr. Johnson, had come to eavesdrop on a meeting of enslaved people, he immediately began to complain of how the masters intended to drive the poor whites away by ordering slaves to shoot their pigs and tear down their fences. This convinced Jones and Johnson that Nat Turner was their friend and the masters were their enemy. They hurried home to protect their property from the wealthy masters.[51]

Such stories illustrate the great power of the trickster tradition in African American thought. After all, one would think that Nat Turner would be the last person to be cast in the role of trickster. Rather, his revolt would appear to represent open confrontation rather than guile. And yet it seems that Turner's absorption into black folk culture included his transformation into a trickster.

Another tradition, common among the black community and sympathetic whites, portrayed Nat Turner as a brilliant freedom fighter and hero. This is the image that appeared in Thomas Wentworth Higginson's article. Higginson referred to Turner as "this extraordinary man," a man who planned "shrewdly," was fearless, and was committed to the freedom of his people. The fugitive from slavery William Wells Brown was a bit more hesitant in his praise, but still enthusiastic. He described Turner as a victim of his own "fanaticism," but also as a brave man who resembled Napoleon in his sense of destiny and who was a "martyr to the freedom of his race."[52] This vision of Turner was continued through the nineteenth and twentieth centuries in the writings of many black and some white novelists, poets, and playwrights.[53]

The image of Nat Turner as freedom fighter also took root within the African American community of Virginia. Evidence of this is difficult to discover because public praise of Turner was dangerous where the white community so passionately despised him. But the praise did surface on occasion. At the August 7, 1867, meeting of the "Colored Shiloh Baptist Association of Virginia," the Cool Spring Baptist Church of Southampton County applied for admission. According to a press report, "Elder Williams requested that the delegates arise, stating that this 'church was located where Nat Turner first struck for freedom.'" The Southampton delegation then "marched forward" with "much shaking of hands and general felicitation."[54] The white community was horrified and shocked by reports of this show of African American respect for Nat Turner. Their strong reaction helps us understand why positive images of Nat Turner so rarely assumed a public form in Virginia. However, this brief glimpse into Virginia African American reaction to Turner's memory indicates the reverence in which he was held by some. Positive images of Nat Turner also emerge during the 1930s in interviews with former Virginia enslaved people.[55]

One of the most famous modern retellings of the Nat Turner story is William Styron's Pulitzer Prize–winning 1967 novel, *The Confessions of Nat Turner*. As with any work of literature, Styron's *Confessions* is not easily summarized. But it does have certain central features worth noting, especially if we are to understand the passionate, racially charged debate that quickly overwhelmed public discussion of the book. Most important, Styron wrote the novel in the voice of Nat Turner. William Styron, a twentieth-century, white, Tidewater Virginia novelist, attempted to imagine the consciousness of a nineteenth century slave and to describe the world through his eyes. Styron's conscious intention was to use Nat Turner's original *Confessions* as a scaffold for the novel. The historical document offered sparse description of the man, and Styron hoped to flesh out the portrait in a way consistent with available evidence about slavery and the rebellion.

Styron saw little merit in the idea that Nat Turner was a brilliant hero willing to give his life for the liberty of his people. As he bluntly phrased it in a 1968 *Yale Literary Magazine* interview, Nat Turner was "a *nut* who gathers together several followers, plows through a county one evening, admittedly without even having devised a plan, and kills fifty-some white people, most of whom are helpless children. *Big deal!* Fine hero."[56] Styron also added a sexual dimension to Nat Turner's life. He gathered together bits of evidence from the documentary record and imagined an erotic life that seemed to fit a pattern he had seen in other revolutionary heroes, such as Gandhi. He noted Turner's ascetic style of life and the fact that he personally killed only a young woman, Margaret Whitehead. Styron believed these clues pointed to a deeply repressed and conflicted sexual longing for a white woman. In the end, Styron implies, it was this twisted sexual desire that drove a vacillating Nat Turner toward rebellion and culminated in the climactic murder of the woman he secretly longed to possess.

While William Styron's *Confessions of Nat Turner* won substantial critical acclaim, it also was attacked with a fury rarely encountered in public academic conversation. The most widely circulated critique appeared in the form of a collection of essays, *William Styron's Nat Turner: Ten Black Writers Respond*, edited and introduced by John Henrik Clarke.[57] This volume included essays by editors and writers Lerone Bennett Jr., Loyle Hairston, Ernest Kaiser, John Oliver Killens, Mike Thelwell, and John A. Williams, political scientist Charles V. Hamilton, historian Vincent Harding, and psychiatrist Alvin F. Poussaint. As a group, the black writers charged Styron with the "deliberate" distortion of the character of the real Nat Turner in order to discredit contemporary freedom fighters in the black community.[58] They argued that Styron's attack on a great black revolutionary of the past was a thinly veiled attack on the black revolutionaries of the present. They pointed to a host of factual errors and fabricated incidents in Styron's novel that transformed the enslaved rebel from noble hero to a weak and hesitant repressed rapist. Styron's own racial-sexual fantasy, they charged, was the real source of Turner's lust for white women. The entire novel, in fact, they said, was the confession of William Styron rather than that of Nat Turner. Styron created a gentle master who taught Turner how to read; he ignored Turner's grandmother, father, and wife; he imagined Turner's mother enjoying rape by a drunken overseer; he invented Turner's hatred for blackness; he transformed Turner into a "house nigger" who masturbated while dreaming of white women; and he failed to understand the power of Turner's religious beliefs and failed to recreate the language, life, and culture of the black community.

The best way to approach the battle over William Styron's novel is to understand that it was a controversy shaped by the politics of the 1960s. A great gulf of misunderstanding and distrust separated Styron and his critics—a gulf that paralleled the sharp racial divisions that then (and still) split American society. Despite his public statement that Turner was a "nut," Styron seems to have consciously intended his novel to be a respectful treatment of the man and his world. Whether or not this was really the case, Styron seems to have believed that his attempt to enter Nat Turner's mind was a racially progressive sign that a major white American novelist would consider the consciousness of a black insurgent worthy of serious attention. Styron did not think of himself as an apologist for racism or the master class. On the contrary, he believed his novel offered a powerful indictment of a horrible institution.

Although he may have been unaware of it, in one sense Styron was writing in the tradition of abolitionist William Lloyd Garrison—deploring the violence of the rebellion but seeing it as a consequence of the institution of slavery. Earlier he had been deeply moved by historian Stanley Elkins's 1959 study, *Slavery: A Problem in American Institutional and Intellectual Life*. Elkins describes a form of slavery so brutal that it devastated the psyche of many blacks. But Styron went beyond Elkins and fleshed out the way close personal, or "paternal," relations between master and slave tortured a human mind and generated extreme violence. In this stress on the close contact between the races, he anticipated Eugene Genovese's now-classic 1974 study of slavery, *Roll, Jordan, Roll*. Genovese, in fact, expressed his strong support for the novel.[59]

Virtually every aspect of Styron's approach to Nat Turner assumed a sinister aspect when seen through the eyes of his critics. Styron's attempt to recreate the consciousness of an enslaved person was not a sign of respect, but an expropriation. In a paraphrase of the Langston Hughes poem that lamented the white theft of the blues from black culture, Vincent Harding entitled his critique "You've Taken My Nat and Gone."[60] The critics saw Styron's attempt to clothe himself in the skin of Nat Turner as a new variation of the old racist blackface tradition in which humiliation and mockery were the goals of whites who imitated blacks. Most important, they did not interpret Styron's portrayal of a damaged black psyche as an attack on the horror of slavery, but as racist stereotyping of black sexuality, family, religion, and heroism. Styron, according to his critics, transformed a strong black hero into a vacillating coward; he changed a man who had died for the freedom of his people into a man who had died for the lust of a white woman; he obliterated the revolt's black roots in a strong and autonomous family and religion and created a new interracial and deeply perverted myth of the rebellion's origin.

Since the William Styron controversy of the 1960s, both academic and popular interest in Nat Turner has ebbed and flowed with the nation's focus on race relations. We have now entered an era of renewed public concern about racial inequality—including concern for inequalities of income and wealth, education, and medical care and the differential racial impact of our criminal justice system. The movement to remind everyone that "black lives matter" has spread across the nation. It should come as no surprise, then, that interest in the history of race relations has likewise been on the increase—and the Nat Turner story remains a vital part of that history.

Until recently, the last major book-length account of the rebellion was published in 1975. In fact, since the dawn of the era of modern scholarship in the late nineteenth century we have had only three major monographic accounts of the rebellion. While we have seen the publication of several edited volumes and individual essays on the subject, or on Nat Turner in American memory, full-length monographic treatments focused on 1831 have been rare.[61] That is why it is so startling to have seen two major new studies published recently: David F. Allmendinger Jr.'s *Nat Turner and the Rising in Southampton* and Patrick H. Breen's *The Land Shall Be Deluged in Blood*. Similarly, in the past there has been a noticeable absence of films about the rebellion. While one major documentary film was broadcast nationally on PBS (*Nat Turner: A Troublesome Property*, written and produced by Charles Burnett, Frank Christopher, and Kenneth S. Greenberg), until recently no one had successfully produced a feature film about Nat Turner. Now, however, a film (written, directed, produced by, and starring Nate Parker) with the provocative title *Birth of a Nation*—a title long associated with one of the most notorious racist films of the early twentieth century—has been released.

D. W. Griffith's original 1915 film told the story of the birth of a nation with white supremacy at its center. Nate Parker's new film tells the story of the birth of a nation with a heroic black rebel at its center. Moreover, the National Museum of African American History and Culture is open at the National Mall in Washington, D.C. Nat Turner's Bible is one of the treasured objects housed in this collection, and the Nat Turner story is now preserved at the literal center of our national memory.

The first edition of this edited *Confessions of Nat Turner* ended with the following thought: "We are ready for a new retelling of the Nat Turner story. Perhaps some reader of this volume will begin the project." It turns out that those words inspired Patrick H. Breen as a student to write one of the two new Nat Turner books just published.[62] It is my hope that one or more among the generation of students now reading this second edition will be moved to retell the Nat Turner story in a way that will excite and inspire future readers.

NOTES

[1]The following summary account of Nat Turner's life is based on *The Confessions of Nat Turner*. All quotations can be found in the *Confessions*.

[2]The *Confessions* contains two versions of how Nat Turner learned to read. In the part of the document written in the voice of Nat Turner, Turner notes, "The manner in which I learned to read and write, not only had great influence on my own mind, as I acquired it with the most perfect ease, so much so, that I have no recollection whatever of learning the alphabet — but to the astonishment of the family, one day, when a book was shewn me to keep me from crying, I began spelling the names of different objects — this was a source of wonder to all in the neighborhood, particularly the blacks. . . ." Later, in the part of the *Confessions* written in the voice of Thomas R. Gray, Gray notes that "he [Nat Turner] can read and write, (it was taught him by his parents,)." The voice of Nat Turner emphasized the supernatural and awe-inspiring nature of his acquisition of literacy. The voice of Thomas R. Gray transformed it into a natural phenomenon. Henry Irving Tragle, ed., *Southampton Slave Revolt of 1831: A Compilation of Source Material* (Amherst: University of Massachusetts Press, 1971), 307, 317.

[3]David F. Allmendinger Jr., *Nat Turner and the Rising in Southampton County* (Baltimore: Johns Hopkins University Press, 2014), 25–43, offers the most complete description of the property transfers that moved Nat Turner from owner to owner.

[4]This biblical quotation was a slight distortion of Matthew 6:33 (KJV): "But seek ye first the kingdom of God and his righteousness; and all these things shall be added unto you."

[5]Allmendinger, *Nat Turner*, 281–82, contains the most careful and complete listing of the names of the insurgents.

[6]Ibid., 159.

[7]Eric Foner, ed., *Nat Turner* (Englewood Cliffs, N.J.: Prentice-Hall, 1971), 3.

[8]Stephen B. Oates, *The Fires of Jubilee: Nat Turner's Fierce Rebellion* (New York: New American Library, 1975), 1–3.

[9]Tragle, ed., *Southampton Slave Revolt*, 14–15; Daniel W. Crofts, *Old Southampton: Politics and Society in a Virginia County, 1834–1869* (Charlottesville: University Press of Virginia, 1992), 11–38.

[10]Tragle, ed., *Southampton Slave Revolt*, 14.

[11]Anthony E. Kaye, "Neighborhoods and Nat Turner: The Making of a Slave Rebel and the Unmaking of a Slave Rebellion," *Journal of the Early Republic* 27, no. 4 (Winter 2007): 705–20. See also Kaye's larger study of the importance of neighborhoods for the slave community throughout the South: Anthony E. Kaye, *Joining Places: Slave Neighborhoods in the Old South* (Chapel Hill: University of North Carolina Press, 2007).

[12]The circulation figure of 40,000 to 50,000 has largely been accepted by historians, but it may only be a very rough approximation or even a guess. The 50,000 figure was first cited in *The Richmond Compiler* and later in Thomas Wentworth Higginson's 1861 essay about the insurrection in *The Atlantic Monthly*. In a later reprint of the article, he changed the figure to 40,000. Higginson offered no documentary support for either figure. However, it does seem likely that the pamphlet achieved wide circulation. The insurrection generated great popular interest, and the pamphlet was reprinted at least twice. See the discussion in Tragle, ed., *Southampton Slave Revolt*, 327, and in Allmendinger, *Nat Turner*, 275.

[13]Thomas C. Parramore, *Southampton County, Virginia* (Charlottesville: University Press of Virginia for the Southampton County Historical Society, 1978), 105–7; Eric J. Sundquist, *To Wake the Nations: Race in the Making of American Literature* (Cambridge, Mass.: Belknap Press of Harvard University Press, 1993), 38; Allmendinger, *Nat Turner*, 216–20, 235.

[14]Seymour L. Gross and Eileen Bender, "History, Politics and Literature: The Myth of Nat Turner," *American Quarterly* 23 (October 1971), 493, have also noted the framing words used by Gray.

[15]Ibid., 497–98.

[16]Henry Irving Tragle, "Styron and His Sources," reprinted in Tragle, ed., *Southampton Slave Revolt*, 397–414. The discussion of the September 17 letter can be found on pages 406–9. See also David F. Allmendinger Jr., "The Construction of *The Confessions of Nat Turner*," in Kenneth S. Greenberg, ed., *Nat Turner: A Slave Rebellion in History and Memory* (New York: Oxford University Press, 2003), 32–34; and Allmendinger, *Nat Turner*, 235–38.

[17]Patrick H. Breen, *The Land Shall Be Deluged in Blood: A New History of the Nat Turner Revolt* (Oxford: Oxford University Press, 2015), 169–70.

[18]Allmendinger, *Nat Turner*, 11–24, 245–53, offers a persuasive argument that most of the *Confessions* is in the voice of Nat Turner and contains much information corroborated by other sources. Breen, *The Land Shall Be Deluged in Blood*, 15–16, 169–79, agrees.

[19]The most thorough recent analysis of the evidence for the existence of Cherry as the wife of Nat Turner can be found in Allmendinger, *Nat Turner*, 63–67. Earlier discussions of Cherry can be found in Oates, *The Fires of Jubilee*, 32–34, 186; and in Tragle, ed., *Southampton Slave Revolt*, 92, 327. The marriage of slaves was not a legal institution in the antebellum South, but slave marriage was commonly sanctioned through ceremony and customary practice. See also Breen, *The Land Shall Be Deluged in Blood*, 194–95, note 9.

[20]Tragle, ed., *Southampton Slave Revolt*, 208. Deborah Gray White, *Ar'n't I a Woman: Female Slaves in the Plantation South* (New York: W. W. Norton, 1985), 70–90, discusses some differences between male and female ways of resisting slavery. Winthrop D. Jordan, *Tumult and Silence at Second Creek: An Inquiry into a Civil War Slave Conspiracy* (Baton Rouge: Louisiana State University Press, 1993), 172–75, has an interesting discussion of the absence of women in American slave rebellions. A good place to find out more about the larger issue of women and resistance to slavery is Stephanie M. H. Camp, *Closer to Freedom: Enslaved Women and Everyday Resistance in the Plantation South* (Chapel Hill: University of North Carolina Press, 2004).

[21]For a discussion of women in the Nat Turner rebellion, see Mary Kemp Davis, "What Happened in This Place: In Search of the Female Slave in the Nat Turner Slave Insurrection," in Greenberg, ed., *Nat Turner*, 162–76.

[22]Allmendinger, *Nat Turner*, 253–57.

[23]For one example of a significant slave rebellion nearly erased from historical memory, see Jordan, *Tumult and Silence at Second Creek*.

[24]Peter Charles Hoffer, *Cry Liberty: The Great Stono River Slave Rebellion of 1739* (Oxford: Oxford University Press, 2010).

[25]On Gabriel's rebellion, see Michael L. Nicholls, *Whispers of Rebellion: Narrating Gabriel's Conspiracy* (Charlottesville: University of Virginia Press, 2012); James Sidbury, *Ploughshares into Swords: Race, Rebellion and Identity in Gabriel's Virginia, 1730–1810* (Cambridge: Cambridge University Press, 1997); and Douglas R. Egerton, *Gabriel's Rebellion: The Virginia Slave Conspiracies of 1800 and 1802* (Chapel Hill: University of North Carolina Press, 1993). The 1811 Louisiana Rebellion is described in Daniel Rasmussen, *American Uprising: The Untold Story of America's Largest Slave Revolt* (New York: Harper-Collins, 2011). On Denmark Vesey, see David Robertson, *Denmark Vesey: The Buried Story of America's Largest Slave Rebellion and the Men Who Led It* (New York: Vintage Books, 2000); and Douglas R. Egerton, *He Shall Go Out Free: The Lives of Denmark Vesey* (Madison, Wis.: Madison House Publishers, 1999).

[26]Eugene D. Genovese, *From Rebellion to Revolution: Afro-American Slave Revolts in the Making of the Modern World* (New York: Vintage Books, 1979); Peter Kolchin, *Unfree Labor: American Slavery and Russian Serfdom* (Cambridge, Mass.: Harvard University Press, 1987), 241–301.

[27]For a summary of the literature on resistance to slavery, see Kenneth S. Greenberg, "Slave Resistance," in *Understanding and Teaching American Slavery*, ed. Bethany Jay and Cynthia Lynn Lyerly (Madison: University of Wisconsin Press, 2016), 133–43.

[28]William Styron, *The Confessions of Nat Turner* (New York: Random House, 1967).

[29]Of course, a modern reader should be a bit skeptical about Nat Turner's denial of links beyond Southampton County. Both Turner and Gray had powerful incentives to emphasize the isolation of the rebels. Turner would not have wanted to implicate others once the rebellion had collapsed. Gray wanted to assure his white Southern readers that there was only one Nat Turner and that his death meant they could retain slavery without fear. Still, no evidence has yet surfaced to indicate that the Nat Turner rebellion had any direct connections outside the county. The best account of the influence of David Walker's *Appeal* can be found in Peter P. Hinks, *To Awaken My Afflicted Brethren: David Walker and the Problem of Antebellum Slave Resistance* (University Park: Pennsylvania State University Press, 1997).

[30]Vincent Harding, *There Is a River: The Black Struggle for Freedom in America* (New York: Random House, 1983), 94, 88.

[31]Lawrence Levine, *Black Culture and Black Consciousness: Afro-American Folk Thought from Slavery to Freedom* (New York: Oxford University Press, 1977), 75–77.

[32]Mechal Sobel, *Trabelin' On: The Slave Journey to an Afro-Baptist Faith* (Princeton, N.J.: Princeton University Press, 1988), 161–66.

[33]Genovese, *From Rebellion to Revolution*.

[34]Harding, *There Is a River*, xii.

[35]Allmendinger, *Nat Turner*, 209; "The Diary of Governor John Floyd," in Tragle, ed., *Southampton Slave Revolt*, 252.

[36]Tragle, ed., *Southampton Slave Revolt*, 253.

[37]Genovese, *From Rebellion to Revolution*, 105–10, notes that in virtually every American slave revolt the brutality of the repression far exceeded the brutality of the rebels. Evidence of the "extrajudicial" killing of African Americans after the Nat Turner rebellion can be found in *The Richmond Compiler*, September 3, 1831, reprinted in Tragle, ed., *Southampton Slave Revolt*, 62; and *The Constitutional Whig*, August 29 and September 3, 1831, reprinted in Tragle, ed., *Southampton Slave Revolt*, 52, 69. See also Oates, *The Fires of Jubilee*, 114. The most recent description and analysis of the slaughter of African Americans in the aftermath of the rebellion can be found in Allmendinger, *Nat Turner*, 203–7. Allmendinger's conclusion that at least twenty-four African Americans were murdered in the aftermath of the rebellion can be found on page 297.

[38]William Sidney Drewry, *The Southampton Insurrection* (Washington, D.C.: Neale Company, 1900), 102. For a fuller discussion of what happened to Nat Turner's body after his death, see Kenneth S. Greenberg, "Name, Face, Body," in Greenberg, ed., *Nat Turner*, 3–23.

[39] *The Richmond Enquirer*, November 8, 1831, reprinted in Tragle, ed., *Southampton Slave Revolt*, 137. In the *Confessions*, Nat Turner himself contended that universal slaughter was only a temporary tactic: "[U]ntil we had armed and equipped ourselves, and gathered sufficient force, neither age nor sex was to be spared." The Ezekiel quotation can be found in Oates, *The Fires of Jubilee*, 78.

[40]See the order of commanding officer F. M. Boykin in *The Lynchburg Virginian*, September 8, 1831, reprinted in Tragle, ed., *Southampton Slave Revolt*, 74–75. Breen, *The Land Shall Be Deluged in Blood*, 107–38, makes the argument that the slaveholder elite of the county shaped the trials to assure the angry white population that the rebellion was local and small-scale—and not a general threat to their way of life. Hence the trials helped calm down an angry white population on the edge of undertaking the slaughter of enslaved people on an even more massive scale.

[41]The trial process is described in Allmendinger, *Nat Turner*, 229–35.

[42]Thomas V. Parramore, *Southampton County, Virginia* (Charlottesville: University Press of Virginia, 1978), 116. Tragle, ed., *Southampton Slave Revolt*, 229–45, includes a summary chart of the results of the trials, with minor errors. For examples of recommended commutation, see pages 181, 198, 221. The trial process is described in Allmendinger, *Nat Turner*, 229–35. The best description of the trials can be found in Breen, *The Land Shall Be Deluged in Blood*.

[43]Daniel W. Crofts, *Old Southampton: Politics and Society in a Virginia County, 1834–1869* (Charlottesville: University Press of Virginia, 1992), 17; Alison Goodyear Freehling, *Drift toward Dissolution: The Virginia Slavery Debate of 1831–1832* (Baton Rouge: Louisiana State University Press, 1982), 193.

[44]Governor John Floyd's November 19, 1831, letter to Governor James Hamilton Jr. is published in Tragle, ed., *Southampton Slave Revolt*, 275–76.

[45]Freehling, *Drift toward Dissolution*, 188–89, 193. On religion in Nat Turner's Virginia, see Randolph Ferguson Scully, *Religion and the Making of Nat Turner's Virginia: Baptist Community and Conflict, 1740–1840* (Charlottesville: University of Virginia Press, 2008). On the substantial, more general, literature on African American Christianity, a good place to begin is Albert J. Raboteau, *Slave Religion: The "Invisible Institution" in the Antebellum South* (New York: Oxford University Press, 1978).

[46]A good description of the Randolph plan can be found in Freehling, *Drift toward Dissolution*, 129–30.

[47]Thomas R. Dew, "Abolition of Negro Slavery," *American Quarterly Review* 7 (1832): 189–265; Thomas R. Dew, *Review of the Debate in the Virginia Legislature of 1831 and 1832* (Richmond, Va.: T. W. White, 1832); *The Pro-Slavery Argument as Maintained by the Most Distinguished Writers of the Southern States* (Charleston, S.C.: Walker, Richards, 1852), 287–490.

[48]See, for example, Joseph C. Robert, *The Road from Monticello: A Study of the Virginia Slavery Debate of 1832* (New York: AMS Press, 1970).

[49] *The Liberator*, September 3, 1831, reprinted in Tragle, ed., *Southampton Slave Revolt*, 62–64. The Henry Highland Garnet speech is quoted in David E. Swift, *Black Prophets of Justice: Activist Clergy before the Civil War* (Baton Rouge: Louisiana State University Press, 1989), 135.

[50]Levine, *Black Culture and Black Consciousness*, 102–35.

[51]Thomas Wentworth Higginson, "Nat Turner's Insurrection," *Atlantic Monthly*, August 1861, 173–87.

[52]William Wells Brown, *The Negro in the American Revolution: His Heroism and His Fidelity* (Boston: Lee and Shepard, 1867), 19–25.

[53]An excellent recent summary and analysis of the wide variety of ways that Nat Turner has been remembered in American culture can be found in Scot French, *The Rebellious Slave: Nat Turner in American Memory* (Boston: Houghton Mifflin, 2004). See also Greenberg, ed., *Nat Turner*.

[54]The description of this incident and all the quotations can be found in Crofts, *Old Southampton*, 243.

[55]Charles L. Perdue Jr., Thomas E. Barden, and Robert K. Phillips, eds., *Weevils in the Wheat: Interviews with Virginia Ex-Slaves* (Bloomington: Indiana University Press, 1980), 35, 67, 75–76.

[56]Douglas Barzelay and Robert Sussman, "William Styron on *The Confessions of Nat Turner:* A *Yale Lit* Interview," *Yale Literary Magazine* 137 (Fall 1968): 24–35. The quote is from a reprint of the article in James L. W. West III, ed., *Conversations with William Styron* (Jackson: University of Mississippi Press, 1985), 100. Styron offered a similar statement at the 1968 American Historical Association convention. There he presented a summary of his understanding of Eugene Genovese's view of Nat Turner as a "perhaps psychotic fanatic, a religious fanatic who, lacking any plan or purpose . . . takes five or six rather bedraggled followers and goes off on a ruthless, directionless, aimless, forty-eight-hour rampage of total destruction, in which the victims are, by a large majority, women and children." Quoted in Albert E. Stone, *The Return of Nat Turner: History, Literature, and Cultural Politics in Sixties America* (Athens: University of Georgia Press, 1992), 13.

[57]John Henrik Clarke, ed., *William Styron's Nat Turner: Ten Black Writers Respond* (Boston: Beacon Press, 1968).

[58]Clarke wrote in his introduction, "The contributors to this book collectively maintain that the distortion of the true character of Nat Turner was deliberate. The motive for this distortion would be William Styron's reaction to the racial climate that has prevailed in the United States in the last fifteen years." Clarke, ed., *William Styron's Nat Turner,* viii.

[59]Styron's discussion of his purposes and intentions can be found in West, ed., *Conversations with William Styron.* For Genovese's ideas on the novel, see Eugene D. Genovese, "The Nat Turner Case," *New York Review of Books,* September 12, 1968, 34–37; and Vincent Harding and Eugene Genovese, "An Exchange on Nat Turner," *New York Review of Books,* November 7, 1968, 35–37.

[60]Vincent Harding, "You've Taken My Nat and Gone," in Clarke, ed., *William Styron's Nat Turner,* 23.

[61]The three significant book-length studies of Nat Turner during the twentieth century are Drewry, *The Southampton Insurrection* (1900); Herbert Aptheker, *Nat Turner's Slave Rebellion* (written as a master's essay in 1937 but not published until 1966); and Oates, *The Fires of Jubilee* (1975).

[62]Breen, *The Land Shall Be Deluged in Blood,* 165.

PART TWO

The Confessions of Nat Turner

THE

CONFESSIONS

OF

NAT TURNER,

THE LEADER OF THE LATE

INSURRECTION IN SOUTHAMPTON, VA.

As fully and voluntarily made to

THOMAS R. GRAY,

In the prison where he was confined, and acknowledged by
him to be such when read before the Court of Southampton; with the certificate, under seal of
the Court convened at Jerusalem,
Nov. 5, 1831, for his trial.

ALSO, AN AUTHENTIC

ACCOUNT OF THE WHOLE INSURRECTION,

WITH LISTS OF THE WHITES WHO WERE MURDERED,

AND OF THE NEGROES BROUGHT BEFORE THE COURT OF SOUTHAMPTON, AND THERE SENTENCED, &c.

Baltimore:

PUBLISHED BY THOMAS R. GRAY.

Lucas & Deaver, print.

1831.

DISTRICT OF COLUMBIA, TO WIT:

Be it remembered, That on this tenth day of November, Anno Domini, eighteen hundred and thirty-one, Thomas R. Gray of the said District, deposited in this office the title of a book, which is in the words as following:

"The Confessions of Nat Turner, the leader of the late insurrection in Southampton, Virginia, as fully and voluntarily made to Thomas R. Gray, in the prison where he was confined, and acknowledged by him to be such when read before the Court of Southampton; with the certificate, under seal, of the Court convened at Jerusalem, November 5,1831, for his trial. Also, an authentic account of the whole insurrection, with lists of the whites who were murdered, and of the negroes brought before the Court of Southampton, and there sentenced, &c. the right whereof he claims as proprietor, in conformity with an Act of Congress, entitled "An act to amend the several acts respecting Copy Rights."

EDMUND J. LEE, Clerk of the District.

(Seal.)

In testimony that the above is a true copy, from the record of the District Court for the District of Columbia, I, Edmund I. Lee, the Clerk thereof, have hereunto set my hand and affixed the seal of my office, this 10th day of November, 1831.

EDMUND J. LEE, C. D. C.

To the Public

The late insurrection in Southampton has greatly excited the public mind, and led to a thousand idle, exaggerated and mischievous reports. It is the first instance in our history of an open rebellion of the slaves, and attended with such atrocious circumstances of cruelty and destruction, as could not fail to leave a deep impression, not only upon the minds of the community where this fearful tragedy was wrought, but throughout every portion of our country, in which this population is to be found. Public curiosity has been on the stretch to understand the origin and progress of this dreadful conspiracy, and the motives which influences its diabolical actors. The insurgent slaves had all been destroyed, or apprehended, tried and executed, (with the exception of the leader,) without revealing any thing at all satisfactory, as to the motives which governed them, or the means by which they expected to accomplish their object. Every thing connected with this sad affair was wrapt in mystery, until Nat Turner, the leader of this ferocious band, whose name has resounded throughout our widely extended empire, was captured. This "great Bandit" was taken by a single individual, in a cave near the residence of his late owner, on Sunday, the thirtieth of October, without attempting to make the slightest resistance, and on the following day safely lodged in the jail of the County. His captor was Benjamin Phipps, armed with a shot gun well charged. Nat's only weapon was a small light sword which he immediately surrendered, and begged that his life might be spared. Since his confinement, by permission of the jailor, I have had ready access to him, and finding that he was willing to make a full and free confession of the origin, progress and consummation of the insurrectory movements of the slaves of which he was the contriver and head; I determined for the gratification of public curiosity to commit his statements to writing, and publish them, with little or no variation, from his own words. That this is a faithful record of his confessions, the annexed certificate of the County Court of Southampton, will attest. They certainly bear one stamp of truth and sincerity. He makes no attempt (as all the other insurgents who were examined did,) to exculpate himself, but frankly acknowledges his full participation in all the guilt of the transaction. He was not only the contriver of the conspiracy, but gave the first blow towards its execution.

It will thus appear, that whilst every thing upon the surface of society wore a calm and peaceful aspect; whilst not one note of preparation was heard to warn the devoted inhabitants of woe and death, a gloomy fanatic was revolving in the recesses of his own dark, bewildered, and overwrought mind, schemes of indiscriminate massacre to the whites. Schemes too fearfully executed as far as his fiendish band proceeded in their desolating march. No cry for mercy penetrated their flinty bosoms. No acts of remembered kindness made the least impression upon these remorseless murderers. Men, women and children, from hoary age to helpless infancy were involved in the same cruel fate. Never did a band of savages do their work of death more unsparingly. Apprehension for their own personal safety seems to have been the only principle of restraint in the whole course of their bloody proceedings. And it is not the least remarkable feature in this horrid transaction, that a band actuated by such hellish purposes, should have resisted so feebly, when met by the whites in arms. Desperation alone, one would think, might have led to greater efforts. More than twenty of them attacked Dr. Blunt's house on Tuesday morning, a little before day-break, defended by two men and three boys. They fled precipitately at the first fire; and their future plans of mischief, were entirely disconcerted and broken up. Escaping thence, each individual sought his own safety either in concealment, or by returning home, with the hope that his participation might escape detection, and all were shot down in the course of a few days, or captured and brought to trial and punishment. Nat has survived all his followers, and the gallows will speedily close his career. His own account of the conspiracy is submitted to the public, without comment. It reads an awful, and it is hoped, a useful lesson, as to the operations of a mind like his, endeavoring to grapple with things beyond its reach. How it first became bewildered and confounded, and finally corrupted and led to the conception and perpetration of the most atrocious and heart-rending deeds. It is calculated also to demonstrate the policy of our laws in restraint of this class of our population, and to induce all those entrusted with their execution, as well as our citizens generally, to see that they are strictly and rigidly enforced. Each particular community should look to its own safety, whilst the general guardians of the laws, keep a watchful eye over all. If Nat's statements can be relied on, the insurrection in this county was entirely local, and his designs confided but to a few, and these in his immediate vicinity. It was not instigated by motives of revenge or sudden anger, but the results of long deliberation, and a settled purpose of mind. The offspring of gloomy fanaticism, acting upon materials but too well prepared for such impressions. It will be long remembered in the annals of our country, and many a mother as she presses her infant darling to her bosom, will shudder at the recollection of Nat Turner, and his band of ferocious miscreants.

Believing the following narrative, by removing doubts and conjectures from the public mind which otherwise must have remained, would give general satisfaction, it is respectfully submitted to the public by their ob't serv't,

T. R. GRAY.

Jerusalem, Southampton, Va. Nov. 5, 1831.

We the undersigned, members of the Court convened at Jerusalem, on Saturday, the 5th day of Nov. 1831, for the trial of Nat, *alias* Nat Turner, a negro slave, late the property of Putnam Moore, deceased, do hereby certify, that the confessions of Nat, to Thomas R. Gray, was read to him in our presence, and that Nat acknowledged the same to be full, free, and voluntary; and that furthermore, when called upon by the presiding Magistrate of the Court, to state if he had any thing to say, why sentence of death should not be passed upon him, replied he had nothing further than he had communicated to Mr. Gray. Given under our hands and seals at Jerusalem, this 5th day of November, 1831.

JEREMIAH COBB,	[*Seal.*]
THOMAS PRETLOW,	[*Seal.*]
JAMES W. PARKER,	[*Seal.*]
CARR BOWERS,	[*Seal.*]
SAMUEL B. HINES,	[*Seal.*]
ORRIS A. BROWNE,	[*Seal.*]

State of Virginia, Southampton County, to wit:

I, James Rochelle, Clerk of the County Court of Southampton in the State of Virginia, do hereby certify, that Jeremiah Cobb, Thomas Pretlow, James W. Parker, Carr Bowers, Samuel B. Hines, and Orris A. Browne, esqr's are acting Justices of the Peace, in and for the County aforesaid, and were members of the Court which convened at Jerusalem, on Saturday the 5th day of November, 1831, for the trial of Nat *alias* Nat Turner, a negro slave, late the property of Putnam Moore, deceased, who was tried and convicted, as an insurgent in the late insurrection in the county of Southampton aforesaid, and that full faith and credit are due, and ought to be given to their acts as Justices of the peace aforesaid.

In testimony whereof, I have hereunto set my hand and caused the seal of the Court [Seal.] aforesaid, to be affixed this 5th day of November, 1831.

JAMES ROCHELLE, C. S. C. C.

Confession

Agreeable to his own appointment, on the evening he was committed to prison, with permission of the jailer, I visited NAT on Tuesday the 1st November, when, without being questioned at all, he commenced his narrative in the following words: —

SIR, — You have asked me to give a history of the motives which induced me to undertake the late insurrection, as you call it — To do so I must go back to the days of my infancy, and even before I was born. I was thirty-one years of age the 2d of October last, and born the property of Benj. Turner, of this county. In my childhood a circumstance occurred which made an indelible impression on my mind, and laid the ground work of that enthusiasm, which has terminated so fatally to many, both white and black, and for which I am about to atone at the gallows. It is here necessary to relate this circumstance — trifling as it may seem, it was the commencement of that belief which has grown with time, and even now, sir, in this dungeon, helpless and forsaken as I am, I cannot divest myself of. Being at play with other children, when three or four years old, I was telling them something, which my mother overhearing, said it had happened before I was born — I stuck to my story, however, and related somethings which went, in her opinion, to confirm it — others being called on were greatly astonished, knowing that these things had happened, and caused them to say in my hearing, I surely would be a prophet, as the Lord had shewn me things that had happened before my birth. And my father and mother strengthened me in this my first impression, saying in my presence, I was intended for some great purpose, which they had always thought from certain marks on my head and breast — [a parcel of excrescences which I believe are not at all uncommon, particularly among negroes, as I have seen several with the same. In this case he has either cut them off or they have nearly disappeared] — My grandmother, who was very religious, and to whom I was much attached — my master, who belonged to the church, and other religious persons who visited the house, and whom I often saw at prayers, noticing the singularity of my manners, I suppose, and my uncommon intelligence for a child, remarked I had too much sense to be raised, and if I was, I would never be of any service to any one as a slave—To a mind like mine, restless, inquisitive and observant of every thing that was passing, it is easy to suppose that religion was the subject to which it would be directed, and although this subject principally occupied my thoughts—there was nothing that I saw or heard of to which my attention was not directed—The manner in which I learned to read and write, not only had great influence on my own mind, as I acquired it with the most perfect ease, so much so, that I have no recollection whatever of learning the alphabet—but to the astonishment of the family, one day, when a book was shewn me to keep me from crying, I began spelling the names of different objects—this was a source of wonder to all in the neighborhood, particularly the blacks—and this learning was constantly improved at all opportunities—when I got large enough to go to work, while employed, I was reflecting on many things that would present themselves to my imagination, and whenever an opportunity occurred of looking at a book, when the school children were getting their lessons, I would find many things that the fertility of my own imagination had depicted to me before; all my time, not devoted to my master's service, was spent either in prayer, or in making experiments in casting different things in moulds made of earth, in attempting to make paper, gunpowder, and many other experiments, that although I could not perfect, yet convinced me of its practicability if I had the means.* I was not addicted to stealing in my youth, nor have ever been—Yet such was the confidence of the negroes in the neighborhood, even at this early period of my life, in my superior judgment, that they would often carry me with them when they were going on any roguery, to plan for them. Growing up among them, with this confidence in my superior judgment, and when this, in their opinions, was perfected by Divine inspiration, from the circumstances already alluded to in my infancy, and which belief was ever afterwards zealously inculcated by the austerity of my life and manners, which became the subject of remark by white and black.—Having soon discovered to be great, I must appear so, and therefore studiously avoided mixing in society, and wrapped myself in mystery, devoting my time to fasting and prayer—By this time, having arrived to man's estate, and hearing the scriptures commented on at meetings, I was struck with that particular passage which says: "Seek ye

---

*When questioned as to the manner of manufacturing those different articles, he was found well informed on the subject.

the kingdom of Heaven and all things shall be added unto you." I
reflected much on this passage, and prayed daily for light on this subject—As I was praying one day at my plough, the spirit spoke to me,
saying "Seek ye the kingdom of Heaven and all things shall be added
unto you." *Question*—what do you mean by the Spirit. *Ans.* The Spirit
that spoke to the prophets in former days—and I was greatly astonished, and for two years prayed continually, whenever my duty would
permit—and then again I had the same revelation, which fully confirmed me in the impression that I was ordained for some great purpose in the hands of the Almighty. Several years rolled round, in which
many events occurred to strengthen me in this my belief. At this time I
reverted in my mind to the remarks made of me in my childhood, and
the things that had been shewn me—and as it had been said of me in
my childhood by those by whom I had been taught to pray, both white
and black, and in whom I had the greatest confidence, that I had too
much sense to be raised, and if I was, I would never be of any use to any
one as a slave. Now finding I had arrived to man's estate, and was a
slave, and these revelations being made known to me, I began to direct
my attention to this great object, to fulfil the purpose for which, by this
time, I felt assured I was intended. Knowing the influence I had obtained
over the minds of my fellow servants, (not by the means of conjuring
and such like tricks—for to them I always spoke of such things with
contempt) but by the communion of the Spirit whose revelations I often
communicated to them, and they believed and said my wisdom came
from God. I now began to prepare them for my purpose, by telling them
something was about to happen that would terminate in fulfilling the
great promise that had been made to me—About this time I was placed
under an overseer, from whom I ran away—and after remaining in the
woods thirty days, I returned, to the astonishment of the negroes on the
plantation, who thought I had made my escape to some other part of
the country, as my father had done before. But the reason of my return
was, that the Spirit appeared to me and said I had my wishes directed to
the things of this world, and not to the kingdom of Heaven, and that
I should return to the service of my earthly master—"For he who
knoweth his Master's will, and doeth it not, shall be beaten with many
stripes, and thus have I chastened you." And the negroes found fault,
and murmured against me, saying that if they had my sense they would
not serve any master in the world. And about this time I had a vision—
and I saw white spirits and black spirits engaged in battle, and the sun
was darkened—the thunder rolled in the Heavens, and blood flowed in
streams—and I heard a voice saying, "Such is your luck, such you are

called to see, and let it come rough or smooth, you must surely bare it." I now withdrew myself as much as my situation would permit, from the intercourse of my fellow servants, for the avowed purpose of serving the Spirit more fully—and it appeared to me, and reminded me of the things it had already shown me, and that it would then reveal to me the knowledge of the elements, the revolution of the planets, the operation of tides, and changes of the seasons. After this revelation in the year 1825, and the knowledge of the elements being made known to me, I sought more than ever to obtain true holiness before the great day of judgment should appear, and then I began to receive the true knowledge of faith. And from the first steps of righteousness until the last, was I made perfect; and the Holy Ghost was with me, and said, "Behold me as I stand in the Heavens"—and I looked and saw the forms of men in different attitudes—and there were lights in the sky to which the children of darkness gave other names than what they really were—for they were the lights of the Saviour's hands, stretched forth from east to west, even as they were extended on the cross on Calvary for the redemption of sinners. And I wondered greatly at these miracles, and prayed to be informed of a certainty of the meaning thereof—and shortly afterwards, while laboring in the field, I discovered drops of blood on the corn as though it were dew from heaven—and I communicated it to many, both white and black, in the neighborhood—and I then found on the leaves in the woods hieroglyphic characters, and numbers, with the forms of men in different attitudes, portrayed in blood, and representing the figures I had seen before in the heavens. And now the Holy Ghost had revealed itself to me, and made plain the miracles it had shown me—For as the blood of Christ had been shed on this earth, and had ascended to heaven for the salvation of sinners, and was now returning to earth again in the form of dew—and as the leaves on the trees bore the impression of the figures I had seen in the heavens, it was plain to me that the Saviour was about to lay down the yoke he had borne for the sins of men, and the great day of judgment was at hand. About this time I told these things to a white man, (Etheldred T. Brantley) on whom it had a wonderful effect—and he ceased from his wickedness, and was attacked immediately with a cutaneous eruption, and blood ozed from the pores of his skin, and after praying and fasting nine days, he was healed, and the Spirit appeared to me again, and said, as the Saviour had been baptised so should we be also—and when the white people would not let us be baptised by the church, we went down into the water together, in the sight of many who reviled us, and were baptised by the Spirit—After this I rejoiced greatly, and gave thanks to God. And on the 12th of May, 1828, I heard a loud noise in the heavens, and the Spirit instantly appeared to me and said the Serpent was loosened, and Christ had laid down the yoke he had borne for the sins of men, and that I should take it on and fight against the Serpent, for the time was fast approaching when the first should be last and the last should be first. *Ques.* Do you not find yourself mistaken now? *Ans.* Was not Christ crucified. And by signs in the heavens that it would make known to me when I should commence the great work—and until the first sign appeared, I should conceal it from the knowledge of men—And on the appearance of the sign, (the eclipse of the sun last February) I should arise and prepare myself, and slay my enemies with their own weapons. And immediately on the sign appearing in the heavens, the seal was removed from my lips, and I communicated the great work laid out for me to do, to four in whom I had the greatest confidence. (Henry, Hark, Nelson, and Sam)—It was intended by us to have begun the work of death on the 4th July last—Many were the plans formed and rejected by us, and it affected my mind to such a degree, that I fell sick, and the time passed without our coming to any determination how to commence—Still forming new schemes and rejecting them, when the sign appeared again, which determined me not to wait longer.

Since the commencement of 1830, I had been living with Mr. Joseph Travis, who was to me a kind master, and placed the greatest confidence in me; in fact, I had no cause to complain of his treatment to me. On Saturday evening, the 20th of August, it was agreed between Henry, Hark and myself, to prepare a dinner the next day for the men we expected, and then to concert a plan, as we had not yet determined on any. Hark, on the following morning, brought a pig, and Henry brandy, and being joined by Sam, Nelson, Will and Jack, they prepared in the woods a dinner, where, about three o'clock, I joined them.

Q. Why were you so backward in joining them.

A. The same reason that had caused me not to mix with them for years before.

I saluted them on coming up, and asked Will how came he there, he answered, his life was worth no more than others, and his liberty as dear to him. I asked him if he thought to obtain it? He said he would, or loose his life. This was enough to put him in full confidence. Jack, I knew, was only a tool in the hands of Hark, it was quickly agreed we should commence at home (Mr. J. Travis') on that night, and until we had armed and equipped ourselves, and gathered sufficient force, neither age nor sex was to be spared, (which was invariably adhered to.) We remained at the feast, until about two hours in the night, when we went to the house and found Austin; they all went to the cider press and drank, except myself. On returning to the house, Hark went to the door with an axe, for the purpose of breaking it open, as we knew we were strong enough to murder the family, if they were awaked by the noise; but reflecting that it might create an alarm in the neighborhood, we determined to enter the house secretly, and murder them whilst sleeping. Hark got a ladder and set it against the chimney, on which I ascended, and hoisting a window, entered and came down stairs, unbarred the door, and removed the guns from their places. It was then observed that I must spill the first blood. On which, armed with a hatchet, and accompanied by Will, I entered my master's chamber, it being dark, I could not give a death blow, the hatchet glanced from his head, he sprang from the bed and called his wife, it was his last word, Will laid him dead, with a blow of his axe, and Mrs. Travis shared the same fate, as she lay in bed. The murder of this family, five in number, was the work of a moment, not one of them awoke; there was a little infant sleeping in a cradle, that was forgotten, until we had left the house and gone some distance, when Henry and Will returned and killed it; we got here, four guns that would shoot, and several old muskets, with a pound or two of powder. We remained some time at the barn, where we paraded; I formed them in a line as soldiers, and after carrying them through all the manœvres I was master of, marched them off to Mr. Salathul Francis', about six hundred yards distant. Sam and Will went to the door and knocked. Mr. Francis asked who was there, Sam replied it was him, and he had a letter for him, on which he got up and came to the door; they immediately seized him, and dragging him out a little from the door, he was dispatched by repeated blows on the head; there was no other white person in the family. We started from there for Mrs. Reese's, maintaining the most perfect silence on our march, where finding the door unlocked, we entered, and murdured Mrs. Reese in her bed, while sleeping; her son awoke, but it was only to sleep the sleep of death, he had only time to say who is that, and he was no more. From Mrs. Reese's we went to Mrs. Turner's, a mile distant, which we reached about sunrise, on Monday morning. Henry, Austin, and Sam, went to the still, where, finding Mr. Peebles, Austin shot him, and the rest of us went to the house; as we approached, the family discovered us, and shut the door. Vain hope! Will, with one stroke of his axe, opened it, and we entered and found Mrs. Turner and Mrs. Newsome in the middle of a room, almost frightened to death. Will immediately killed Mrs. Turner, with one blow of his axe. I took Mrs. Newsome by the hand, and with the sword I had when I was apprehended, I struck her several blows over the head, but not being able to kill her, as the sword was dull. Will turning around and discovering it, despatched her also. A general destruction of property and search for money and ammunition, always succeeded the murders. By this time my company amounted to fifteen, and nine men mounted, who started for Mrs. Whitehead's, (the other six were to go through a by way to Mr. Bryant's, and rejoin us at Mrs. Whitehead's,) as we approached the house we discovered Mr. Richard Whitehead standing in the cotton patch, near the lane fence; we called him over into the lane, and Will, the executioner, was near at hand, with his fatal axe, to send him to an untimely grave. As we pushed on to the house, I discovered some one run round the garden, and thinking it was some of the white family, I pursued them, but finding it was a servant girl belonging to the house, I returned to commence the work of death, but they whom I left, had not been idle; all the family were already murdered, but Mrs. Whitehead and her daughter Margaret. As I came round to the door I saw Will pulling Mrs. Whitehead out of the house, and at the step he nearly severed her head from her body, with his broad axe. Miss Margaret, when I discovered her, had concealed herself in the corner, formed by the projection of the cellar cap from the house; on my approach she fled, but was soon overtaken, and after repeated blows with a sword, I killed her by a blow on the head, with a fence rail. By this time, the six who had gone by Mr. Bryant's, rejoined us, and informed me they had done the work of death assigned them. We again divided, part going to Mr. Richard Porter's, and from thence to Nathaniel Francis', the others to Mr. Howell Harris', and Mr. T. Doyles. On my reaching Mr. Porter's, he had escaped with his family. I understood there, that the alarm had already spread, and I immediately returned to bring up those sent to Mr. Doyles, and Mr. Howell Harris'; the party I left going on to Mr. Francis', having told them I would join them in that neighborhood. I met these sent to Mr. Doyles' and Mr. Harris' returning, having met Mr. Doyle on the road and killed him; and learning from some who joined them, that Mr. Harris was from home, I immediately pursued the course taken by the party gone on before; but knowing they would complete the work of death and pillage, at Mr. Francis' before I could get there, I went to Mr. Peter Edwards', expecting to find them there, but they had been here also. I then went to Mr. John T. Barrow's, they had been here and murdered him. I pursued on their track to Capt. Newit Harris', where I found the greater part mounted, and ready to start; the men now amounting to about forty, shouted and hurraed as I rode up, some were in the yard, loading their guns, others drinking. They said Captain Harris and his family had escaped, the property in the house they destroyed, robbing him of money and other valuables. I ordered them to mount and march instantly, this was about nine or ten o'clock, Monday morning. I proceeded to Mr. Levi Waller's two or three miles distant. I took my station in the rear, and as it 'twas my object to carry terror and devastation wherever we went, I placed fifteen or twenty of the best armed and most to be relied on, in front, who generally approached the house as fast as their horses could run; this was for two purposes, to prevent their escape and strike terror to the inhabitants—on this account I never got to the houses, after leaving Mrs. Whitehead's, until the murders were committed, except in one case. I sometimes got in sight in time to see the work of death completed, viewed the mangled bodies as they lay, in silent satisfaction, and immediately started in quest of other victims—Having murdered Mrs. Waller and ten children, we started for Mr. William Williams'—having killed him and two little boys that were there; while engaged in this, Mrs. Williams fled and got some distance from the house, but she was pursued, overtaken, and compelled to get up behind one of the company, who brought her back, and after showing her the mangled body of her lifeless husband, she was told to get down and lay by his side, where she was shot dead. I then started for Mr. Jacob Williams, where the family were murdered—Here we found a young man named Drury, who had come on business with Mr. Williams—he was pursued, overtaken and shot. Mrs. Vaughan was the next place we visited—and after murdering the family here, I determined on starting for Jerusalem—Our number amounted now to fifty or sixty, all mounted and armed with guns, axes, swords and clubs—On reaching Mr. James W. Parkers' gate, immediately on the road leading to Jerusalem, and about three miles distant, it was proposed to me to call there, but I objected, as I knew he was gone to Jerusalem, and my object was to reach there as soon as possible; but some of the men having relations at Mr. Parker's it was agreed that they might call and get his people. I remained at the gate on the road, with seven or eight; the others going across the field to the house, about half a mile off. After waiting some time for them, I became impatient, and started to the house for them, and on our return we were met by a party of white men, who had pursued our blood-stained track, and who had fired on those at the gate, and dispersed them, which I new nothing of, not having been at that time rejoined by any of them—Immediately on discovering the whites, I ordered my men to halt and form, as they appeared to be alarmed—The white men, eighteen in number, approached us in about one hundred yards, when one of them fired, (this was against the positive orders of Captain Alexander P. Peete, who commanded, and who had directed the men to reserve their fire until within thirty paces). And I discovered about half of them retreating, I then ordered my men to fire and rush on them; the few remaining stood their ground until we approached within fifty yards, when they fired and retreated. We pursued and overtook some of them who we thought we left dead; (they were not killed) after pursuing them about two hundred yards, and rising a little hill, I discovered they were met by another party, and had haulted, and were re-loading their guns, (this was a small party from Jerusalem who knew the negroes were in the field, and had just tied their horses to await their return to the road, knowing that Mr. Parker and family were in Jerusalem, but knew nothing of the party that had gone in with Captain Peete; on hearing the firing they immediately rushed to the spot and arrived just in time to arrest the progress of these barbarous villians, and save the lives of their friends and fellow citizens.) Thinking that those who retreated first, and the party who fired on us at fifty or sixty yards distant, had all only fallen back to meet others with amunition. As I saw them re-loading their guns, and more coming up than I saw at first, and several of my bravest men being wounded, the others became panick struck and squandered over the field; the white men pursued and fired on us several times. Hark had his horse shot under him, and I caught another for him as it was running by me; five or six of my men were wounded, but none left on the field; finding myself defeated here I instantly determined to go through a private way, and cross the Nottoway river at the Cypress Bridge, three miles below Jerusalem, and attack that place in the rear, as I expected they would look for me on the other road, and I had a great desire to get there to procure arms and amunition. After going a short distance in this private way, accompanied by about twenty men, I overtook two or three who told me the others were dispersed in every direction. After tyring [*sic*] in vain to collect a sufficient force to proceed to Jerusalem, I determined to return, as I was sure they would make back to their old neighborhood, where they would rejoin me, make new recruits, and come down again. On my way back, I called at Mrs. Thomas's, Mrs. Spencer's, and several other places, the white families having fled, we found no more victims to gratify our thirst for blood, we stopped at Majr. Ridley's quarter for the night, and being joined by four of his men, with the recruits made since my defeat, we mustered now about forty strong. After placing out sentinels, I laid down to sleep, but was quickly roused by a great racket; starting up, I found some mounted, and others in great confusion; one of the sentinels having given the alarm that we were about to be attacked, I ordered some to ride round and reconnoitre, and on their return the others being more alarmed, not knowing who they were, fled in different ways, so that I was reduced to about twenty again; with this I determined to attempt to recruit, and proceed on to rally in the neighborhood, I had left. Dr. Blunt's was the nearest house, which we reached just before day; on riding up the yard, Hark fired a gun. We expected Dr. Blunt and his family were at Maj. Ridley's, as I knew there was a company of men there; the gun was fired to ascertain if any of the family were at home; we were immediately fired upon and retreated, leaving several of my men. I do not know what became of them, as I never saw them afterwards. Pursuing our course back and coming in sight of Captain Harris', where we had been the day before, we discovered a party of white men at the house, on which all deserted me but two, (Jacob and Nat,) we concealed ourselves in the woods until near night, when I sent them in search of Henry, Sam, Nelson, and Hark, and directed them to rally all they could, at the place we had had our dinner the Sunday before, where they would find me, and I accordingly returned there as soon as it was dark and remained until Wednesday evening, when discovering white men riding around the place as though they were looking for some one, and none of my men joining me, I concluded Jacob and Nat had been taken, and compelled to betray me. On this I gave up all hope for the present; and on Thursday night after having supplied myself with provisions from Mr. Travis's, I scratched a hole under a pile of fence rails in a field, where I concealed myself for six weeks, never leaving my hiding place but for a few minutes in the dead of night to get water which was very near; thinking by this time I could venture out, I began to go about in the night and eaves drop the houses in the neighborhood; pursuing this course for about a fortnight and gathering little or no intelligence, afraid of speaking to any human being, and returning every morning to my cave before the dawn of day. I know not how long I might have led this life, if accident had not betrayed me, a dog in the neighborhood passing by my hiding place one night while I was out, was attracted by some meat I had in my cave, and crawled in and stole it, and was coming out just as I returned. A few nights after, two negroes having started to go hunting with the same dog, and passed that way, the dog came again to the place, and having just gone out to walk about, discovered me and barked, on which thinking myself discovered, I spoke to them to beg concealment. On making myself known they fled from me. Knowing then they would betray me, I immediately left my hiding place, and was pursued almost incessantly until I was taken a fortnight afterwards by Mr. Benjamin Phipps, in a little hole I had dug out with my sword, for the purpose of concealment, under the top of a fallen tree. On Mr. Phipps' discovering the place of my concealment, he cocked his gun and aimed at me. I requested him not to shoot and I would give up, upon which he demanded my sword. I delivered it to him, and he brought me to prison. During the time I was pursued, I had many hair breadth escapes, which your time will not permit you to relate. I am here loaded with chains, and willing to suffer the fate that awaits me.

I here proceeded to make some inquiries of him, after assuring him of the certain death that awaited him, and that concealment would only bring destruction on the innocent as well as guilty, of his own color, if he knew of any extensive or concerted plan. His answer was, I do not. When I questioned him as to the insurrection in North Carolina happening about the same time, he denied any knowledge of it; and when I looked him in the face as though I would search his inmost thoughts, he replied, "I see sir, you doubt my word; but can you not think the same ideas, and strange appearances about this time in the heaven's might prompt others, as well as myself, to this undertaking." I now had much conversation with and asked him many questions, having forborne to do so previously, except in the cases noted in parenthesis; but during his statement, I had, unnoticed by him, taken notes as to some particular circumstances, and having the advantage of his statement before me in writing, on the evening of the third day that I had been with him, I began a cross examination, and found his statement corroborated by every circumstance coming within my own knowledge or the confessions of others whom had been either killed or executed, and whom he had not seen nor had any knowledge since 22d of August last, he expressed himself fully satisfied as to the impracticability of his attempt. It has been said he was ignorant and cowardly, and that his object was to murder and rob for the purpose of obtaining money to make his escape. It is notorious, that he was never known to have a dollar in his life; to swear an oath, or drink a drop of spirits. As to his ignorance, he certainly never had the advantages of education, but he can read and write, (it was taught him by his parents,) and for natural intelligence and quickness of apprehension, is surpassed by few men I have ever seen. As to his being a coward, his reason as given for not resisting Mr. Phipps, shews the decision of his character. When he saw Mr. Phipps present his gun, he said he knew it was impossible for him to escape as the woods were full of men; he therefore thought it was better to surrender, and trust to fortune for his escape. He is a complete fanatic, or plays his part most admirably. On other subjects he possesses an uncommon share of intelligence, with a mind capable of attaining any thing; but warped and perverted by the influence of early impressions. He is below the ordinary stature, though strong and active, having the true negro face, every feature of which is strongly marked. I shall not attempt to describe the effect of his narrative, as told and commented on by himself, in the condemned hole of the prison. The calm, deliberate composure with which he spoke of his late deeds and intentions, the expression of his fiend-like face when excited by enthusiasm, still bearing the stains of the blood of helpless innocence about him; clothed with rags and covered with chains; yet daring to raise his manacled hands to heaven, with a spirit soaring above the attributes of man; I looked on him and my blood curdled in my veins.

I will not shock the feelings of humanity, nor wound afresh the bosoms of the disconsolate sufferers in this unparalleled and inhuman massacre, by detailing the deeds of their fiend-like barbarity. There were two or three who were in the power of these wretches, had they known it, and who escaped in the most providential manner. There were two whom they thought they left dead on the field at Mr. Parker's, but who were only stunned by the blows of their guns, as they did not take time to re-load when they charged on them. The escape of a little girl who went to school at Mr. Waller's, and where the children were collecting for that purpose, excited general sympathy. As their teacher had not arrived, they were at play in the yard, and seeing the negroes approach, she ran up on a dirt chimney, (such as are common to log houses,) and remained there unnoticed during the massacre of the eleven that were killed at this place. She remained on her hiding place till just before the arrival of a party, who were in pursuit of the murderers, when she came down and fled to a swamp, where, a mere child as she was, with the horrors of the late scene before her, she lay concealed until the next day, when seeing a party go up to the house, she came up, and on being asked how she escaped, replied with the utmost simplicity, "The Lord helped her." She was taken up behind a gentleman of the party, and returned to the arms of her weeping mother. Miss Whitehead concealed herself between the bed and the mat that supported it, while they murdered her sister in the same room, without discovering her. She was afterwards carried off, and concealed for protection by a slave of the family, who gave evidence against several of them on their trial. Mrs. Nathaniel Francis, while concealed in a closet heard their blows, and the shrieks of the victims of these ruthless savages; they then entered the closet where she was concealed, and went out without discovering her. While in this hiding place, she heard two of her women in a quarrel about the division of her clothes. Mr. John T. Baron, discovering them approaching his house, told his wife to make her escape, and scorning to fly, fell fighting on his own threshold. After firing his rifle, he discharged his gun at them, and then broke it over the villain who first approached him, but he was overpowered, and slain. His bravery, however, saved from the hands of these monsters, his lovely and amiable wife, who will long lament a husband so deserving of her love. As directed by him, she attempted to escape through the garden, when she was caught and held by one of her servant girls, but another coming to her rescue, she fled to the woods, and concealed herself. Few indeed, were those who escaped their work of death. But fortunate for society, the hand of retributive justice has overtaken them; and not one that was known to be concerned has escaped.

The Commonwealth,
    vs.   Charged with making insurrection,
  Nat Turner.   and plotting to take away the lives of
divers free white persons, &c. on the 22d of August, 1831.

The court composed of——, having met for the trial of Nat Turner, the prisoner was brought in and arraigned, and upon his arraignment pleaded *Not guilty;* saying to his counsel, that he did not feel so.

On the part of the Commonwealth, Levi Waller was introduced, who being sworn, deposed as follows: *(agreeably to Nat's own Confession.)* Col. Trezvant* was then introduced, who being sworn, narrated Nat's Confession to him, as follows: *(his Confession as given to Mr. Gray.)* The prisoner introduced no evidence, and the case was submitted without argument to the court, who having found him guilty, Jeremiah Cobb, Esq. Chairman, pronounced the sentence of the court, in the following words: "Nat Turner! Stand up. Have you any thing to say why sentence of death should not be pronounced against you?

Ans. I have not. I have made a full confession to Mr. Gray, and I have nothing more to say.

Attend then to the sentence of the Court. You have been arraigned and tried before this court, and convicted of one of the highest crimes in our criminal code. You have been convicted of plotting in cold blood, the indiscriminate destruction of men, of helpless women, and of infant children. The evidence before us leaves not a shadow of doubt, but that your hands were often imbrued in the blood of the innocent; and your own confession tells us that they were stained with the blood of a master; in your own language, "too indulgent." Could I stop here, your crime would be sufficiently aggravated. But the original contriver of a plan,

---

*The committing Magistrate.

deep and deadly, one that never can be effected, you managed so far to put it into execution, as to deprive us of many of our most valuable citizens; and this was done when they were asleep, and defenceless; under circumstances shocking to humanity. And while upon this part of the subject I cannot but call your attention to the poor misguided wretches who have gone before you. They are not few in number — they were your bosom associates; and the blood of all cries aloud, and calls upon you, as the author of their misfortune. Yes! You forced them unprepared, from Time to Eternity. Borne down by this load of guilt, your only justification is, that you were led away by fanaticism. If this be true, from my soul I pity you; and while you have my sympathies, I am, nevertheless called upon to pass the sentence of the court. The time between this and your execution, will necessarily be very short; and your only hope must be in another world. The judgment of the court is, that you be taken hence to the jail from whence you came, thence to the place of execution, and on Friday next, between the hours of 10 A. M. and 2 P. M. be hung by the neck until you are dead! dead! dead and may the Lord have mercy upon your soul.

A LIST OF PERSONS MURDERED IN THE INSURRECTION, ON THE 21ST AND 22D OF AUGUST, 1831

Joseph Travers and wife and three children, Mrs. Elizabeth Turner, Hartwell Prebles, Sarah Newsome, Mrs. P. Reese and son William, Trajan Doyle, Henry Bryant and wife and child, and wife's mother, Mrs. Catharine Whitehead, son Richard and four daughters and grandchild, Salathiel Francis, Nathaniel Francis' overseer and two children, John T. Barrow, George Vaughan, Mrs. Levi Waller and ten children, William Williams, wife and two boys, Mrs. Caswell Worrell and child, Mrs. Rebecca Vaughan, Ann Eliza Vaughan, and son Arthur, Mrs. John K. Williams and child, Mrs. Jacob Williams and three children, and Edwin Drury — amounting to fifty-five.

A LIST OF NEGROES BROUGHT BEFORE THE COURT OF SOUTHAMPTON, WITH THEIR OWNERS' NAMES, AND SENTENCE

Name	Owner	Sentence
Daniel,	Richard Porter,	Convicted.
Moses,	J. T. Barrow,	Do.
Tom,	Caty Whitehead,	Discharged.
Jack and Andrew,	Caty Whitehead,	Con. and transported.
Jacob,	Geo. H. Charlton,	Disch'd without trial.
Isaac,	Ditto,	Convi. and transported.
Jack,	Everett Bryant,	Discharged.
Nathan,	Benj. Blunt's estate,	Convicted.

Nathan, Tom, and Davy, (boys,)	Nathaniel Francis,	Convicted and transported.
Davy,	Elizabeth Turner,	Convicted.
Curtis,	Thomas Ridley,	Do.
Stephen,	Do.	Do.
Hardy and Isham,	Benjamin Edwards,	Convicted and transp'd.
Sam,	Nathaniel Francis,	Convicted.
Hark,	Joseph Travis' estate.	Do.
Moses, (a boy,)	Do.	Do. and transported
Davy,	Levi Waller,	Convicted.
Nelson,	Jacob Williams,	Do.
Nat,	Edm'd Turner's estate,	Do.
Jack,	Wm. Reese's estate,	Do.
Dred,	Nathaniel Francis,	Do.
Arnold, Artist, (free,)		Discharged.
Sam,	J. W. Parker,	Acquitted.
Ferry and Archer,	J. W. Parker,	Disch'd without trial.
Jim,	William Vaughan,	Acquitted.
Bob,	Temperance Parker,	Do.
Davy,	Joseph Parker,	
Daniel,	Solomon D. Parker,	Disch'd without trial.
Thomas Haithcock, (free,)		Sent on for further trial.
Joe,	John C. Turner,	Convicted.
Lucy,	John T. Barrow,	Do.
Matt,	Thomas Ridley,	Acquitted.
Jim,	Richard Porter,	Do.
Exum Artes, (free,)		Sent on for further trial.
Joe,	Richard P. Briggs,	Disch'd without trial.
Bury Newseome, (free,)		Sent on for further trial.
Stephen,	James Bell,	Acquitted.
Jim and Isaac,	Samuel Champion,	Convicted and trans'd.
Preston,	Hannah Williamson,	Acquitted.
Frank,	Solomon D. Parker,	Convi'd and transp'd.
Jack and Shadrach,	Nathaniel Simmons,	Acquitted.
Nelson,	Benj. Blunt's estate,	Do.
Sam,	Peter Edwards,	Convicted.
Archer,	Arthur G. Reese,	Acquitted.
Isham Turner, (free,)		Sent on for further trial.
Nat Turner,	Putnam Moore, dec'd,	Convicted.

Related Documents

PART THREE

Related Documents

1

The Richmond Compiler
August 24, 1831

This newspaper account was one of the earliest published reports of the rebellion. Such news descriptions were the major way in which information about the revolt spread beyond Southampton County. Typically, antebellum newspapers did not rely on their own staff of reporters to gather information beyond their locality. The editors reprinted other news accounts, spoke to travelers from the scene, or published letters from correspondents closer to the event. Hence, as was the case here, they often published confused or incomplete stories.

One interesting feature of this account is the way the writer assumes, on the basis of no evidence whatsoever, that the rebels must be "mad — infatuated — deceived by some artful knaves, or stimulated by their own miscalculating passions." Also, note the repeated condemnation of "exaggerated" reports. The writer understood that discussing a slave rebellion was a sensitive subject, and he did not want to create panic in the white community.

This city was thrown into some excitement yesterday in consequence of a report in circulation that there was some insurrection of negroes in the county of Southampton. We have made it our business to trace these reports and we have ascertained the following facts:

An express was despatched by Col. Trezvant with a short letter dated on the 21st purporting to be for the *information of the public*, and addressed to the Authorities of the town of Petersburg, stating that an insurrection had broken out among the blacks; that several white families had been destroyed; that arms and ammunition were wanting in Southampton; and that a considerable military force might be required to subdue the disturbers. Colonel Trezvant resides in the town of Jerusalem, in Southampton County — and it would seem that the disturbance had arisen in another part of the county, and that his very general

---

The Richmond Compiler, Richmond, Virginia, August 24, 1831.

statement was forwarded on rumour, which, as in other cases, we suspect, will prove much exaggerated. The letter does not state the names of the families, that are said to have been destroyed, nor the number of the blacks concerned, nor anything which can shed any light upon the character of the transaction. The letter of Col. Trezevant was evidently written in great haste—it required some little time to decypher it. To remove any sort of doubt of its authenticity, Mr. Gilliam of Petersburg had certified that he knew Col. T's hand writing and that it was genuine.

It is reported that when this letter was received, the Petersburg Volunteers immediately put themselves in march for the scene itself.

The Recorder of the Town, upon receiving the letter despetched it to the Mayor of this City.—A new express arrived in this city with the letter about 3 o'clock on Monday night. Early in the morning the Mayor put it into the hands of the Governor of the Commonwealth, who immediately convened the Council. The Lieutenant Governor, the only member in town, who advised the earliest and most efficient measures to be taken—leaving full direction to the Governor upon the subject. Arrangements were immediately taken by the Chief Magistrate for that purpose. Arms and ammunition were despatched in waggons to the county of Southampton. The four volunteer Companies from Petersburg, two Companies from Richmond (viz: the Cavalry and the Artillery,) one from Norfolk, and one from Portsmouth, and the Regiments of Sussex and Southampton have been ordered out. The Dragoons of this city, commanded by Captain Randolph Harrison (60 or 70 strong) set out in the evening about 5 o'clock, and will probably be on the ground by 12 o'clock. The distance is about 60 miles.

The Lafayette Artillery company, commanded by Captain Richardson, embarked last evening about 8 o'clock, in the steam boat Norfolk, and will land at Smithfield.

The intelligence has burst very unexpectedly upon us. No one has had the slightest intimation or dream of such movement. We have no doubt that the transaction has been much exaggerated; and that less mischief has been done, and less force has been gathered together, than has been rumoured, and that the range of the evil will soon be arrested. The wretches who have conceived this thing are mad—infatuated—deceived by some artful knaves, or stimulated by their own miscalculating passions. The ruin must return on their own heads—they must fall certain sacrifice to their own folly and infatuation.

It is scarcely necessary to say that everything is perfectly quiet here—all our population unusually calm—and that these rumours have not ruffled the tranquility of the city. All our care is for our brethren in Southampton; who, from some local cause or other, not explained or conjectured, have been subjected to this visitation. The authorities of the city are, however, on the alert, as they should be. No danger appears but no necessary caution will be spared—the police will be vigilant. Last night the Richmond Light Infantry Blues were out on the watch—the surveillance will be maintained until our volunteer corps are returned, and tranquility shall be restored to the infected district, if *District* it can be called.

—Since writing the above we understand another express has arrived (about 6 o'clock last evening). He is sent by the Mayor of Petersburg, Mr. Wallace, to the Governor. He writes for arms—these have been accordingly dispatched. He speaks of Col. Trezevant's letter—and refers the Governor to Mr. Blunt, the Express, for the accounts in circulation in Petersburg.—The rumours are that seven of the blacks began with destroying a widow and family in Southampton—but the accounts of their force, designs, etc., are so vague and confused, that we shall not undertake to give them "form and pressure." It was reported that they were on their way to Belfield, in the county of Greensville, not many miles from the borders of North Carolina. This point would locate the insurrection in the Southwest portion of the county of Southampton.

A passenger who arrived last night in the Steamboat Richmond, heard no accounts of this affair at Norfolk—nor from any of the passengers who were taken up at the several points on the river.

We must caution our reader against all exaggerations.—He ought to take *every report* with many grains of allowance—he will scarcely be safe if he believes a fiftieth part of what he hears.

2

The Constitutional Whig
August 29, 1831

*The Constitutional Whig was the only newspaper with a reporter on the
scene. Editor John Hampden Pleasants was a member of a Richmond
militia unit that was sent to Southampton County. He mailed back a
series of dispatches with graphic descriptions of the rebellion. In this
report, Pleasants describes the horror experienced by the militia who first
came upon the scenes of slaughter. He also remarks on the absence of rape
during the rebellion, as well as on the summary executions and decapita-
tions committed by furious whites.*

Extract of a letter from the Senior Editor, dated
    JERUSALEM, Southampton Ct. House
        Thursday Evening, Aug. 25.

The Richmond Troop arrived here this morning a little after 9 o'clock,
after a rapid, hot and most fatiguing march from Richmond. On the
road, we met a thousand different reports, no two agreeing, and leaving
it impossible to make a plausible guess at the truth. On the route from
Petersburg, we found the whole country thoroughly alarmed; every
man armed, the dwellings all deserted by the white inhabitants, and
the farms most generally left in possession of the blacks. On our arrival
at this village, we found Com. Elliot and Col. Worth, with 250 U. States
troops, from the neighborhood of Old Point, and a considerable militia
force. A Troop of Horse from Norfolk and one from Prince George, have
since arrived. Jerusalem was never so crowded from its foundation; for
besides the considerable military force assembled here, the ladies from
the adjacent country, to the number of 3 or 400, have sought refuge
from the appalling dangers by which they were surrounded.

    Here for the first time, we learnt the extent of the insurrection, and
the mischief perpetrated. Rumor had infinitely exaggerated the first,
swelling the numbers of the negroes to a thousand or 1200 men, and
representing its ramifications as embracing several of the adjacent coun-

The Constitutional Whig, Richmond, Virginia, August 29, 1831.

ties, particularly Isle of Wight and Greensville; but it was hardly in the power of rumor itself, to exaggerate the atrocities which have been perpetrated by the insurgents: whole families, father, mother, daughters, sons, sucking babes, and school children, butchered, thrown into heaps, and left to be devoured by hogs and dogs, or to putrify on the spot. At Mr. Levi Waller's, his wife and ten children, were murdered and piled in one bleeding heap on his floor.—Waller himself was absent at the moment, but approaching while the dreadful scene was acting, was pursued, and escaped into a swamp, with much difficulty. One small child in the house at the time, escaped by concealing herself in the fire place, witnessing from the place of her concealment, the slaughter of the family, and her elder sisters among them. Another child was cruelly wounded and left for dead, and probably will not survive. All these children were not Mr. Waller's. A school was kept near his house, at which, and between which and his house, the ruthless villains murdered several of the helpless children. Many other horrors have been perpetrated. The killed, as far as ascertained, amount to sixty-two; I send a list believed to be correct, as far as it goes. There are probably others not yet known hereafter to be added. A large proportion of these were women and children. It is not believed that any outrages were offered to the females.

How, or with whom, the insurrection originated, is not certainly known. The prevalent belief is, that on Sunday week last, at Barnes' Church in the neighborhood of the Cross Keys, the negroes who were observed to be disorderly, took offence at something; (it is not known what) that the plan of insurrection was then and there conceived, matured in the course of the week following, and carried into execution on Sunday night the 21st August. The atrocities commenced at Mr. Travis'. A negro, called captain Moore, and who it is added is a preacher, is the reputed leader. On Monday, most of the murders were perpetrated. It is said, that none have been committed since that day. The numbers engaged are not supposed to have exceeded 60—one account says a hundred—another not so many as 40. Twelve armed and resolute men, were certainly competent to have quelled them at any time. But, taken by surprise—with such horrors before their eyes, and trembling for their wives and children, the men, most naturally, only thought in the first place of providing a refuge for those dependent upon them. Since this has been effected, the citizens have acted with vigor. Various parties have scoured the country, and a number of the insurgents, (differently reported,) have been killed or taken. There are thirteen prisoners now at this place, one or more of them severely wounded; the principal of them, a man aged about 21, called Marmaduke, who might have been a hero, judging from the magnanimity with which he bears his sufferings. He is said to be an atrocious offender, and the murderer of Miss Vaughan, celebrated for her beauty. The Preacher-Captain has not been taken. At the Cross Keys, summary justice in the form of decapitation has been executed on one or more prisoners. The people are naturally enough, wound up to a high pitch of rage, and precaution is even necessary to protect the lives of the captives — scouring parties are out, and the insurrection may be considered as already suppressed.

JERUSALEM, Saturday 27.

Since writing the accompanying letter, which was expected to have been sent off immediately, other prisoners have been taken, and in one or two instances, put to death forthwith by the enraged inhabitants. Some of these scenes are hardly inferior in barbarity to the atrocities of the insurgents; and it is to be feared that a spirit of vindictive ferocity has been excited, which may be productive of farther outrage, and prove discreditable to the country. Since Monday, the insurgent negroes have committed no aggression, but have been dodging about in the swamps, in parties of three and four. They are hunted by the local militia with great implacability, and must all eventually, be slain or made captive. All the mischief was done between Sunday morning and Monday noon. In this time, the rebels traversed a country of near 20 miles extent, murdering every white indiscriminately, and wrecking the furniture. They set fire to no houses, and as far as is known, committed no outrage on any white female. What the ulterior object was, is unknown. The more intelligent opinion is that they had none; though some of them say it was to get to Norfolk, seize a ship and go to Africa. My own impression is, that they acted under the influence of their leader Nat, a preacher and a prophet among them; that even he had no ulterior purpose, but was stimulated exclusively by fanatical revenge, and perhaps misled by some hallucination of his imagined spirit of prophecy. — Committing the first murder, finding themselves already beyond the reach of pardon, drunk and desperate, they proceeded in blind fury, to murder and destroy all before them. It will be long before the people of this country can get over the horrors of the late scenes, or feel safe in their homes. — Many will probably migrate. It is an aggravation of the crimes perpetrated, that the owners of slaves in this country are distinguished for lenity and humanity. Cotton and corn are the staples here, and the labor of attending to these is trifling compared with what is necessary in other parts of the State.

3

The Richmond Enquirer
August 30, 1831

This account included more detail about the revolt. Many of these particulars were confirmed later in Nat Turner's description of the insurrection.

The Banditti

So much curiosity has been excited in the state, and so much exaggeration will go abroad, that we have determined to devote a great portion of this day's paper to the strange events in the county of Southampton. . . . What strikes us as the most remarkable thing in this matter is the horrible ferocity of these monsters. They remind one of a parcel of bloodthirsty wolves rushing down from the Alps; or, rather like a former incursion of the Indians upon the white settlements. Nothing is spared; neither age nor sex is respected—the helplessness of women and children pleads in vain for mercy. The danger is thought to be over—but prudence still demands precaution. The lower country should be on the alert.—The case of Nat Turner warns us. No black man ought to be permitted to turn a Preacher through the country. The law must be enforced or the tragedy of Southampton appeals to us in vain. . . .

Extract of a letter from Jerusalem, Va., 24th August, 3 o'clock
"The oldest inhabitants of our county, have never experienced such a distressing time, as we have had since Sunday night last. The negroes, about fifteen miles above this place, have massacred from 50 to 75 women and children, and some 8 or 10 men. Every house, room and corner in this place is full of women and children, driven from home, who had to take [to] the wood[s,] until they could get to this place. We are worn out with fatigue." . . .

Excerpt from the Richmond Compiler, August 29, 1831
A fanatic preacher by the name of Nat Turner (Gen. Nat Turner) who had been taught to read and write, and permitted to go about preaching

---

The Richmond Enquirer, Richmond, Virginia, August 30, 1831.

in the country, was at the bottom of this infernal brigandage. He was artful, impudent and vindicative, without any cause or provocation, that could be assigned.—He was the slave of Mr. Travis. He and another slave of Mr. T. a young fellow, by the name of Moore, were two of the leaders. Three or four others were first concerned and most active.—They had 15 others to join them. And by importunity or threats they prevailed upon about 20 others to cooperate in the scheme of massacre. We cannot say how long they were organizing themselves—but they turned out on last Monday morning early (the 22d) upon their nefarious expedition. . . . They were mounted to the number of 40 or 50; and with knives and axes—knocking on the head, or cutting the throats of their victims. They had few fire-arms among them—and scarcely one, if one, was fit for use . . . But as they went from house to house, they drank ardent spirits—and it is supposed, that in consequence of their being intoxicated, or from mere fatigue, they paused in their murderous career about 12 o'clock on Monday.

A fact or two, before we continue our narrative. These wretches are now estimated to have committed *sixty-one murders!* Not a white person escaped at all the houses they visited except *two*. One was a little child at Mrs. Waller's, about 7 or 8 years of age, who had sagacity enough to creep up a chimney; and the other was Mrs. Barrow, whose husband was murdered in his cotton patch, though he had received some notice in the course of the morning of the murderous deeds that were going on; but placed no confidence in the story and fell victim to his incredul[i]ty. His wife hid herself between weather-boarding of the room, and the un-plastered lathing, and escaped, the wretches not taking time to hunt her out. It was believed that one of the brigands had taken up a spite against Mr. Barrow, because he had refused him one of his female slaves for a wife.

Early on Tuesday morning, they attempted to renew their bloody work.—They made an attack upon Mr. Blunt, a gentleman who was very unwell with the gout, and who instead of flying, determined to brave them out. He had several pieces of fire-arms, perhaps seven or eight, and he put them into the hands of his own slaves, who nobly and gallantly stood by him. They repelled the brigands—killed one, wounded and took prisoner (Gen. Moore), and we believe took a third who was not wounded at all. . . .

Excerpt from dispatch by General Eppes, August 29, 1831
Nat, the ring-leader, who calls himself General, pretends to be a Baptist preacher—a great enthusiast—declares to his comrades that he is commissioned by Jesus Christ, and proceeds under his inspired direc-

tions—that the late singular appearance of the Sun was the sign for him, etc., etc., is among the number not yet taken. The story of his having been killed at the bridge near Jerusalem, and of two engagements there, is unfounded. It is believed he cannot escape.

The General [the militia commander] is convinced, from various sources of information, that there existed no general concert among the slaves.—Circumstances, impossible to have been feigned, demonstrate the entire ignorance on the subject, of all the slaves in the counties around Southampton, among whom he has never known more perfect order and quiet to prevail.

4

The Liberator

September 3, 1831

This editorial was written by Boston abolitionist William Lloyd Garrison. His newspaper, The Liberator, *first appeared on January 1, 1831, and some Southerners suggested that it could have inspired the Nat Turner rebellion. Garrison denied that his words produced the horror of revolt. Instead, he placed the blame on hypocritical masters—men who brutalized their slaves and simultaneously proclaimed their love of liberty.*

What we have so long predicted,—at the peril of being stigmatized as an alarmist and declaimer,—has commenced its fulfilment. The first step of the earthquake, which is ultimately to shake down the fabric of oppression, leaving not one stone upon another, has been made. The first drops of blood, which are but the prelude to a deluge from the gathering clouds, have fallen. The first flash of the lightning, which is to smite and consume, has been felt. The first wailings of a bereavement, which is to clothe the earth in sackcloth, have broken upon our ears.

In the first number of the Liberator, we alluded to the hour of vengeance in the following lines:

Wo if it come with storm, and blood, and fire,
　　When midnight darkness veils the earth and sky!
Wo to the innocent babe—the guilty sire—
　　Mother and daughter—friends of kindred tie!
　　Stranger and citizen alike shall die!
Red-handed Slaughter his revenge shall feed,
　　And Havoc yell his ominous death-cry,
And wild Despair in vain for mercy plead—
While hell itself shall shrink and sicken at the deed!

Read the account of the insurrection in Virginia, and say whether our prophecy be not fulfilled. What was poetry—imagination—in January, is now a bloody reality. "Wo to the innocent babe—to mother and daughter!" Is it not true? Turn again to the record of slaughter! Whole families have been cut off—not a mother, not a daughter, not a babe left. Dreadful retaliation! "The dead bodies of white and black lying just as they were slain, unburied"—the oppressor and the oppressed equal at last in death—what a spectacle!

True, the rebellion is quelled. Those of the slaves who were not killed in combat, have been secured, and the prison is crowded with victims destined for the gallows!

Yet laugh not in your carnival of crime
Too proudly, ye oppressors!

You have seen, it is to be feared, but the beginning of sorrows. All the blood which has been shed will be required at your hands. At your hands alone? No—but at the hands of the people of New-England and of all the free states. The crime of oppression is national. The south is only the agent in this guilty traffic. But, remember! the same causes are at work which must inevitably produce the same effects; and when the contest shall have again begun, it must be again a war of extermination. In the present instance, no quarters have been asked or given.

But we have killed and routed them now—we can do it again and again—we are invincible! A dastardly triumph, well becoming a nation of oppressors. Detestable complacency, that can think, without emotion, of the extermination of the blacks! We have the power to kill *all*—let us, therefore, continue to apply the whip and forge new fetters!

In his fury against the revolters, who will remember their wrongs? What will it avail them, though the catalogue of their sufferings, dripping with warm blood fresh from their lacerated bodies, be held up to extenuate their conduct? It is enough that the victims were black—that circumstance makes them less precious than the dogs which have been slain in our streets! They were black—brutes, pretending to be men—legions of curses upon their memories! They were black—God made them to serve us!

Ye patriotic hypocrites! ye panegyrists of Frenchmen, Greeks, and Poles! ye fustian[1] declaimers for liberty! ye valiant sticklers for equal rights among yourselves! ye haters of aristocracy! ye assailants of monarchies! ye republican nullifiers! ye treasonable disunionists! be dumb! Cast no reproach upon the conduct of the slaves, but let your lips and cheeks wear the blisters of condemnation!

Ye accuse the pacific friends of emancipation of instigating the slaves to revolt. Take back the charge as a foul slander. The slaves need no incentives at our hands. They will find them in their stripes—in their emaciated bodies—in their ceaseless toil—in their ignorant minds—in every field, in every valley, on every hill-top and mountain, wherever you and your fathers have fought for liberty—in your speeches, your conversations, your celebrations, your pamphlets, your newspapers—voices in the air, sounds from across the ocean, invitations to resistance above, below, around them! What more do they need? Surrounded by such influences, and smarting under their newly made wounds, is it wonderful[2] that they should rise to contend—as other "heroes" have contended—for their lost rights? It is *not* wonderful.

In all that we have written, is there aught to justify the excesses of the slaves? No. Nevertheless, they deserve no more censure than the Greeks in destroying the Turks, or the Poles in exterminating the Russians, or our fathers in slaughtering the British. Dreadful, indeed, is the standard erected by worldly patriotism!

For ourselves, we are horror-struck at the late tidings. We have exerted our utmost efforts to avert the calamity. We have warned our countrymen of the danger of persisting in their unrighteous conduct. We have preached to the slaves the pacific precepts of Jesus Christ. We have appealed to christians, philanthropists and patriots, for their assistance to accomplish the great work of national redemption through the agency of moral power—of public opinion—of individual duty. How have we been received? We have been threatened, proscribed, vilified and imprisoned—a laughing-stock and a reproach. Do we falter, in view of these things? Let time answer. If we have been hitherto urgent,

[1]Inflated, bombastic speech.
[2]Surprising.

and bold, and denunciatory in our efforts,—hereafter we shall grow vehement and active with the increase of danger. We shall cry, in trumpet tones, night and day,—Wo to this guilty land, unless she speedily repent of her evil doings! The blood of millions of her sons cries aloud for redress! IMMEDIATE EMANCIPATION can alone save her from the vengeance of Heaven, and cancel the debt of ages!

5

The Constitutional Whig

September 3, 1831

The following account was written by Constitutional Whig *editor John Hampden Pleasants following his return to Richmond after serving with the militia in Southampton County. It deals with several noteworthy topics. Pleasants offers a detailed description of Dr. Blunt's (spelled "Blount" in this article) successful defense of his house, along with an account of the brutal killings at Mrs. Vaughan's residence. Pleasants also was concerned with the problem of panic in the wake of the revolt. He condemns exaggerated newspaper reports, criticizes the slaughter of suspected rebels without a trial, and speculates on whether the rebellion involved a conspiracy that extended beyond the borders of Southampton County.*

Southampton Affair

We have been astonished since our return from Southampton (whither we went with Capt. Harrison's Troop of Horse) in reading over the mass of exchange papers accumulated in our absence, to see the number of false, absurd, and idle rumors, circulated by the Press, touching the insurrection in that county. Editors seem to have applied themselves to the task of alarming the public mind as much as possible by persuading the slaves to entertain a high opinion of their strength and consequences. While truth is always the best policy, and best remedy, the exaggerations to which we have alluded are calculated to give the slaves false conceptions of their numbers and capacity, by exhibiting the terror and confusion of the whites, and to induce them to think that practicable, which they see is so much feared by their superiors.

We have little to say of the Southampton Tragedy beyond what is already known. The origin of the conspiracy, the prime agents, its extent and ultimate direction, is matter of conjecture.—The universal opinion in that part of the country is that Nat, a slave, a preacher, and a pretended prophet was the first [blurred word], the actual leader, and the most remorseless of the executioners. According to the evidence of a negro boy whom they carried along to hold their horses, Nat commenced the scene of murder at the first house (Travis') with his own hand. Having called upon two others to make good their valiant boasting, so often repeated, of what they would do, and these shrinking from the requisition, Nat proceeded to dispatch one of the family with his own hand. Animated by the example and exhortations of their leader, having a taste of blood and convinced that they had now gone too far to recede, his followers dismissed their doubts and became as ferocious as their leader wished them. To follow the [blurred word] capture of Travis' house early that day, to their dispersion at Parker's cornfield early in the afternoon, when they had traversed near 20 miles, murdered 63 whites, and approached within 3 or 4 miles of the Village of Jerusalem; the immediate object of their movement—to describe the scenes at each house, the circumstances of the murders, the hair breadth escapes of the few who were lucky enough to escape—would prove as interesting as heart rending. Many of the details have reached us but not in so authentic a shape as to justify their publication, nor have we the time or space. Let a few suffice. Of the event at Dr. Blount's we had a narrative from the gallant old gentleman himself, and his son, a lad about 15, distinguished for his gallantry and modesty, and whom we take leave to recommend to Gen. Jackson, for a warrant in the Navy or at West Point. The Doctor had received information of the insurrection, and that his house would be attacked a short time before the attack was made. Crippled with the gout, and indisposed to leave, he decided to defend his home. His force was his son, overseer and three other white men. Luckily there were six guns, and plenty of powder and shot in the house. These were barely loaded, his force posted, and the instructions given, when the negroes from 15 to 30 strong, rode up about day break. The Doctor's orders were that each man should be particular in his aim and should fire one at a time; he himself reserved one gun, resolved if the house was forced to sell his life as dearly as he could. The remaining five fired in succession upon the assailants, at the distance of fifteen or twenty steps. The blacks, upon the fifth fire, retreated, leaving one killed (we believe) and one wounded (a fellow named Hark,) and were pursued by the Doctor's negroes with shouts and execrations. Had the shot been larger, more execution doubtless would have been done.

Mrs. Vaughan's was among the last houses attacked. A venerable negro woman described the scene which she had witnessed with great emphasis: it was near noon and her mistress was making some preparations in the porch for dinner, when happening to look towards the road she discerned a dust and wondered what it could mean. In a second, the negroes mounted and armed, rushed into view, and making an exclamation indicative of her horror and agony, Mrs. Vaughan ran into the house.—The negroes dismounted and ran around the house, pointing their guns at the doors and windows. Mrs. Vaughan appeared at a window, and begged for her life, inviting them to take everything she had. The prayer was answered by one of them firing at her, which was followed by another, and a fatal, shot. In the meantime, Miss Vaughan, who was upstairs, and unappraised of the terrible advent until she heard the noise of the attack, rushed down, and begging for her life, was shot as she ran a few steps from the door. A son of Mrs. Vaughan, about 15, was at the still house, when hearing a gun and conjecturing, it is supposed, that his brother had come from Jerusalem, approached the house and was shot as he got over the fence. It is difficult for the imagination to conceive a situation so truly and horribly awful, as that in which these unfortunate ladies were placed. Alone, unprotected, and unconscious of danger, to find themselves without a moment's notice for escape or defence, in the power of a band of ruffians, from whom instant death was the least they could expect! In a most lively and picturesque manner, did the old negress describe the horrors of the scene; the blacks riding up with imprecations, the looks of her mistress, white as a sheet, her prayers for her life, and the actions of the scoundrels environing the house and pointing their guns at the doors and windows, ready to fire as occasion offered. When the work was done they called for drink, and food, and becoming nice, damned the brandy as vile stuff.

The scene at Vaughan's may suffice to give an idea of what was done at the other houses. A bloodier and more accursed tragedy was never acted, even by the agency of the tomahawk and scalping knife. Interesting details will no doubt be evolved in the progress of the trials and made known to the public.

It is with pain we speak of another feature of the Southampton Rebellion; for we have been most unwilling to have our sympathies for the sufferers diminished or affected by their misconduct. We allude to the slaughter of many blacks, without trial, and under circumstances of great barbarity. How many have thus been put into death (generally by decapitation or shooting) reports vary; probably however some five and twenty and from that to 40; possibly a yet larger number. To the great honor of General Eppes, he used every precaution in his power, and we hope and believe with success, to put a stop to the disgraceful procedure.—We met with one individual of intelligence, who stated that he himself had killed between 10 and 15. He justified himself on the grounds of the barbarities committed on the whites; and that he thought himself right is certain from the fact that he narrowly escaped losing his own life in an attempt to save a negro woman whom he thought innocent but who was shot by the multitude in despite of his exertions. We (the Richmond Troop) witnessed with surprise the sanguinary temper of the population who evinced a strong disposition to inflict immediate death on every prisoner. Not having witnessed the horrors committed by the blacks, or seen the unburried and disfigured remains of their wives and children, we were unprepared to understand their feelings, and could not at first admit of their extenuation, which a closer observation of the atrocities of the insurgents suggested. Now, however, we feel individually compelled to offer an apology for the people of Southampton, while we deeply deplore that human nature urged them to such extremities. Let the fact not be doubted by those whom it most concerns, that another such insurrection will be the signal for the extirmination of the whole black population in the quarter of the state where it occurs.

The numbers engaged in the insurrection are variously reported. They probably did not exceed 40 or 50, and were fluctuating from desertions and new recruits. About fifty are in Southampton jail, some of them on suspicion only.—We trust and believe that the intelligent magistracy of the county, will have the firmness to oppose the popular passions, should it be disposed to involve the innocent with the guilty, and to take suspicion for proof.

The presence of the troops from Norfolk and Richmond alone prevented retaliation from being carried much farther.

At the date of Capt. Harrison's departure from Jerusalem, Gen. Nat had not been taken. On that morning, however, Dred, another insurgent chief, was brought prisoner to Jerusalem, having surrendered himself to his master, in the apprehension, no doubt, of starving in the swamps or being shot by the numerous parties of local militia, who were in pursuit. Nat had not certainly been heard from since the skirmish in Parker's cornfield, which was in fact, the termination of the insurrection; the negroes after that dispersing themselves, and making no further attempt. He is represented as a shrewd fellow, reads, writes, and preaches; and by various artificies had acquired great influence over the minds of the wretched beings whom he has led into destruction. It is supposed that he induced them to believe that there were only 80,000 whites in the country, who, being exterminated, the blacks might take possession. Various of his tricks to acquire and preserve influence had been mentioned, but they are not worth repeating. If there was any ulterior purpose, he probably alone knows it. For our own part, we still believe there was none; and if he be the intelligent man represented, we are incapable of conceiving the aruguments by which he persuaded his own mind of the feasibility of his attempt, or how it could possibly end but in certain destruction. We therefore incline to the belief that he acted upon no higher principle that the impulse of revenge against the whites, as the enslavers of himself and his race; that, being a fanatic, he possibly persuaded himself that Heaven would interfere; and that he may have convinced himself, as he certainly did his deluded followers to some extent, that the appearance of the sun some weeks ago, prognosticated something favorable to their cause. We are inclined to think that the solar phenomenon exercised considerable influence in promoting the insurrection; calculated as it was to impress the imaginations of the ignorant.

A more important inquiry remains — whether the conspiracy was circumscribed to the neighborhood in which it broke out, or had its ramifications through other counties. We, at first, adopted the first opinion; but there are several circumstances which favor the latter. We understand that the confessions of all the prisoners go to show that the insurrection broke out too soon, as it is supposed, in consequence of the last day of July being a Sunday, and not, as the negroes in Southampton believed, the Saturday before. The report is that the rising was fixed for the fourth Sunday in August, and that they supposing Sunday, the 31st of July to be the first Sunday in August, they were betrayed into considering the 3d Sunday as the 4th. This is the popular impression founded upon confessions, upon the indications of an intention of the negroes in Nansemond and other places to unite, and upon the allegation that Gen. Nat extended his preaching excursions to Petersburg and this city; allegations which we, however, disbelieve. It is more than probable, nevertheless, that the mischief was concerted and concocted under the cloak of religion. The trials which are now proceeding in Southampton, Sussex, and elsewhere, will develop all the truth. We suspect the truth will turn out to be that the conspiracy was confined to Southampton, and that the idea of its extensiveness originated in the panic which seized upon the South East of Virginia.

6

The Richmond Enquirer
September 20, 1831

This account contains information about the trials of some of the rebels. It also refers to the trials of suspected insurrectionists in other counties.

The Banditti

We understand that accounts have been received by the Governor from Southampton, that the Court has adjourned, and twenty-one slaves have been condemned; of those, nine have been recommended for reprieve and transportation; three being boys of 14 or 15 years of age and all of them being forced to join the band of murderers. Some of the twelve have been already executed, and others remain for execution. The military force has been disbanded, with the exception of a small force of about seventeen men, who assist in guarding the jail, and will continue in service until all the executions have taken place.

Thirty or forty slaves have been tried or examined in Nansemond, but only one has been sentenced to death. It is said that *he* was present at a meeting of the blacks; at which a black preacher (from the Isle of Wight or Surrey) had asked such as were willing to join, to hold up their hands—this fellow was identified as one of those who held up their hands.

We understand that eight or nine convictions have taken place in the county of Sussex. And in Prince George, a black preacher, and by trade a blacksmith, has also been sentenced to death. . . .

We had an unpleasant rumor on Sunday, about the murder of an old lady, two young ones, and two maid servants, in the county of Dinwiddie.

The Richmond Enquirer, Richmond, Virginia, September 20, 1831.

But it turns out to be all a *hoax,* or rather *a dream*. Many of the militia had proceeded to the scene before the hoax was discovered. . . .

The accounts from our Sister State of *North Carolina* have been very much exaggerated; though as they relate to the designs and plans of the Banditti, they are of a more serious complexion. The Raleigh and Warrenton papers, which reached us on Saturday, teemed with very unpleasant accounts—as for instance, according to the P.S. of the Warrenton paper, that Wilmington had been burnt, its inhabitants massacred, and that a large force, swelled up to 2000, was on the march for Raleigh. All these reports turn out to be "the mere coinage of the brain," and it is now exceedingly questionable whether a single black has been under arms. It is certain that not a drop of white man's blood has been shed.

7

The Constitutional Whig

September 26, 1831

This article includes a letter that is one of the most complete accounts of the insurrection written before the publication of the Confessions. *Some historians have concluded that the form and language of this letter suggest it was written by Thomas R. Gray, the man who would later transcribe and structure Nat Turner's confessions. Others disagree. Readers should note that it contains one of the few indications that Nat Turner was married.*

We publish, today a detailed account of the late insurrection in Southampton, kindly furnished us by a gentleman well conversant with the scenes he describes, and fully competent, from the sources of information he possesses, to arrive at a correct conclusion, as to the causes which prompted the ringleader, and the end he had in view. The writer's speculations are therefore, deserving serious consideration, and we are very much inclined to concur with him in the opinion, that it was a sudden and unprepared outbreak of fanaticism and subtle craft, wholly

The Constitutional Whig, Richmond, Virginia, September 26, 1831.

unconnected with any concert in neighboring counties. We expressed our belief, of the contrary, when we heard the other day of the reported atrocious murders in North Carolina, but upon more mature reflection, we are now convinced, that we founded our opinions then, too hastily, upon the exaggerated account before us, and which we did not suppose could receive so general a belief, and so apparently an authentic shape, without a foundation in truth.

We owe the writer an apology, for the liberty we have taken, in abridging his remarks. Necessity compelled us to do so, or want of room, would have entirely excluded him. We have, however, taken care to omit no facts, related by him, and of these, the reader will find many new, and throwing much light on the shocking occurrence.

JERUSALEM, Sept. 17, 1831

Messrs. Editors: Being firmly convinced, that the public would be gratified by a detailed account, of the late unfortunate occurrence in our county; and likewise conscious, that justice to the innocent requires, that the causes, the extent, and number of persons involved in the late insurrection, should be correctly understood, I have resolved to enter upon the task.—Professional duties prevent me, from bestowing as much attention to the drawing up of this narrative as I would wish.—And I must therefore, submit it to the public crude and undigested; sketched *amid* scenes, but ill calculated, to support me in my opinions.—Another inducement, exclusive of any sanctioned by humanity, is, that there are so many rumors afloat, and so many misstatements in the public prints, that a sacred duty to my country, demands a correct view of this tragedy.

It is only since the affair appears to be settled, that I have thought seriously upon the subject.—In almost every section of our county, conversation instead of being as it was a month since, light and cheerful, is now cloathed in dismal forebodings.—Some of our citizens will leave us—and all agree, that they never again can feel safe, never again be happy. But let us examine into their apprehensions, and see if we can administer no comfort.

* * *

I have heard many express their fears of a general insurrection, they are ignorant who believe in the possibility of such a thing.—What the relative proportion of black to white is, in the slaveholding states I know not—having no means of obtaining correct information at this time; but suppose the proponderance to be in favour of the blacks to any extent; and you cannot create causes for alarm. Is it possible for men, debased degraded as they are, ever to concert effective measures? Would the *slaves* alone in St. Domingo ever have attempted insurrection? I humbly apprehend not. It was the march of intellect among the free blacks, that first gave impulse to the tide, which poured its torrents throughout the Island.—Can any person entertain serious apprehensions from this portion of our population; situated as they are—without arms, without concert, what can be effected? Why nothing—and a serious attempt, will never be made while they are thus situated.

* * *

But if any desire there was to increase this spirit among our slaves, I would advise our citizens, to permit coloured preachers to go on, as they have for several years past haranging vast crowds, when and where they pleased, the character of their sermons known only to their congregations—Nor do I think some of our white brethren, exempt from censure, when they fill their discourses with a *ranting cant* about equality.—If our insurrection was known, beyond the neighborhood of its commencement—its cause must be attributed to the misguided zeal of good men, preaching up equality; and to ignorant blacks, who again retail the same doctrine, with such comments, as their heated imaginations may supply, to their respective circles of acquaintance.—For my own part, I think when a minister goes into a pulpit, flies into a passion, beats his fist, and in fine, plays the bloackhead, that he gives a warrant to any negro who hears him, to do whatever he pleases provided his imagination, can make God sanction it.—If the insurrection was general, it is fortunate, that it happened at this time.—For if it had been delayed longer the minds of the blacks would have been better prepared, the plot more extensive, and consequently the carnage much greater. But believing it highly improbable, that a serious attempt will ever be made while they remain in their present state of ignorance; satisfied that no general concert, can ever be effected, unless by the means of education; and conscious from the advantage of the whites over the blacks in moral firmness, that an attempt under any circumstances, would be futile and frivolous, I feel perfectly easy.

But I would caution all missionaries, who are bettering the condition of the world, and all philanthropists, who have our interest so much at stake, not to plague themselves about our slaves but leave them exclusively to our own management. The only possible crisis, in which our slaves can ever become formidable, is in the event of civil wars.

Our insurrection. [*sic*] general, or not, was the work of fanaticism—*General Nat* was no preacher, but in his immediate neighbourhood, he had acquired the character of a prophet; like a Roman Sybil,[1] he traced his divination in characters of blood, on leaves alone in the woods; he would arrange them in some conspicuous place, have a dream telling him of the circumstance; and then send some ignorant black to bring them to him, to whom he would interpret their meaning. Thus, by means of this nature, he acquired an immense influence, over such persons as he took into his confidence.—He, likewise, pretended to have conversations with the Holy Spirit; and was assured by it, that he was invulnerable. His escape, as he laboured under that opinion, is much to be regretted. 'Tis true, that Nat has for some time, thought closely on this subject—for I have in my possession, some papers given up by his wife, under the lash—they are filled with hieroglyphical characters, conveying no definite meaning. The characters on the oldest paper, apparently appear to have been traced with blood; and on each paper, a crucifix and the sun, is distinctly visible; with the figures, 6,000, 30,000, 80,000, &c.—There is likewise a piece of paper, of a late date, which, all agree, is a list of his men; if so, they were short of twenty. I have been credibly informed, that something like three years ago, Nat received a whipping from his master, for saying that the blacks ought to be free, and that they would be free one day or other. Nat in person, is not remarkable, his nose is flat, his stature rather small, and hair very thin, without any peculiarity of expression. As a proof of his shrewdness, he had acquired a great influence over his neighbourhood acquaintance, without being noticed by the whites—pretends to be acquainted with the art of making gunpowder, and likewise that of making paper. My own impression is, he has left the State—many believe him to be yet lurking in his neighbourhood. There are various rumours of having been from home, many days at a time, preaching in Richmond, Petersburg, and Brunswick. They are however, entirely without foundation. The truth is, I have never heard of his preaching any where. He exhorted, and sung at neighborhood meetings, but no farther—To an imagination like Nat's, worked upon for years, by pretended visions; with a mind satisfied of the possibility, of freeing himself and race from bondage; and this by supernatural means. To one thus situated, is it wonderful, that the singular appearance of the sun in August, should have tempted him to execute his purpose: particularly when its *silvery* surface was defaced by a black spot, which Nat interpreted into positive proof, that he would succeed in his undertaking. Nat encouraged his company on their route, by telling them, that as the black spot had passed over the sun, so would the blacks pass over

[1] Prophet, witch, or fortune-teller.

the earth. Having assigned the cause of the insurrection, it becomes necessary to examine its extent. As far back, as a knowledge of this affair, can be attributed to even six or seven, upon credible testimony, is Sunday forenoon, 21st of August, and this credible testimony consists in the declaration of several negroes, supported by collateral circumstances. On Sunday forenoon, the day preceding the fatal Monday; Nat, Austin, Will, Hark, Sam, Henry, and Jack, met in an old field, near Mr. Joseph Travis's, where they had melons, and something to eat. Nat was observed to take them out, one at a time, and hold long conversations with them.

Having developed his plans to each man some brandy was introduced, and the affair talked of together. Even then, one of the party, objected to the proposition, and denied the possibility of effecting it. Nat assured them of its practicability—saying, that their numbers would increase as they went along; and stated, that his reasons for not telling of it before, was, that the negroes had frequently attempted, similar things, confided their purpose to several, and that it always leaked out; but his resolve was, that their march of destruction and murder, should be the first news of the insurrection.

In support of this momentary procedure, I would alledge the fact, that the affair was commenced without a single firelock, and without the least particle of ammunition. Killing the first family with their axes, they then obtained several guns, and some shot. If the design had been thought of for the least length of time, they certainly would have made some preparation. As another proof that it was not general, they did not make one dozen *efficient* recruits, along their whole route of slaughter—they certainly made many more, but instead of being of any service, most of them had to be guarded, by some two or three of the principals, furnished with guns; with orders to shoot the first man, who endeavoured to escape. Many persons have expressed their surprise, how so few could guard so many. To me it appears, that the orders to shoot down whoever attempted to escape, explains the riddle. No one would rashly make the effort, and their situations, prevented any concert for that purpose—so that some no doubt, were forced to remain in company, much longer than they wished, for want of an opportunity to escape—many who were forced away unwillingly, excited by the free use of spirits, became reconciled. But under all circumstances, something like ten; I think not more, could appropriate to themselves exclusively, the performance of every butchery. In support of my opinion, I have examined every source for authentic information. Every individual who was taken alive, has been repeatedly questioned; many of them, when their stay in this world, was exceedingly brief—and the answers of all, confirm me in my belief. It is really amusing, to trace to their sources, many of the rumours, which circulate through our country; and which have fixed public opinion. Leaving out of view, the exaggerated account of the numbers first engaged; we hear of twenty-five stand of arms being found at Brandon—many more at this, that, and the other place—positive evidence of a previous knowledge of insurrection, in all the adjoining counties—Nat preaching in Petersburg, Brunswick, and Richmond—not one word of which, am I able to believe, though I have sought to have it corroborated, from every respectable source. We hear likewise, of a great black preaching near Norfolk, consisting of 500 souls: and the minister, at the close of his discourse, pursuing the plan of Mr. Campbell,[2] calls out to all who are of his way of thinking, to hold up their right hands—all held up their hands but two. Now, all persons who can believe that an insurrection is managed in this way, have more credulity than myself—yet, one of those dissenting two, has identified a black, who was at the aforesaid preaching, and I understand the court of Nansemond, has sentenced him to be hanged. Report says, Norfolk jail is full, upon similar evidence. What the courts will do in that quarter, with the oaths of 498, when weighed with two—I know not.

On the consequences of this rebellion, petty as it is, my opinions are almost exclusively my own; and therefore, it is impolitic to mention them—but of the manner of treating it, together with other subjects, closely connected, I will presently speak.

I must here pay a passing tribute to our slaves, but one which they richly deserve—it is, that there was not an instance of disaffection, in any section of our country; save on the plantations which *Capt. Nat* visited, and to their credit, the recruits were few, and from the chief settlement among them, not a man was obtained.—Many from the course pursued by the negroes, were heard to remark, that if they had to choose a master, it would never be a black one. Had I time, I could detail many an act of true fidelity; but I believe, though the butcheries were inhuman, there was not a single instance of wanton torture.

This view of the subject, leads me to enquire, into *Capt. Nat's* design. His object was freedom and indiscriminate carnage his watchward. The

---

[2]Probably a reference to Alexander Campbell, founder of the Disciples of Christ, a religious group held in contempt by the dominant Protestant denominations.

seizure of Jerusalem, and the massacre of its inhabitants, was with him, a chief purpose, & seemed to be his *ultimatum*; for farther, he gave no clue to his design — possessed of that, he would have thought his object attained. — But a frolick captured *Andrew*,[3] and a frolick saved Jerusalem — *Nat's* object was to commence his butcheries, as soon as the inhabitants of the county were asleep, by that means allowing himself full time, to despatch the citizens on his route; and arrive at this place before day — but several of his party getting beastly drunk, at their dinner on Sunday, delayed until very late in the night his purpose — the seizure however of this place, would have had little other effect than supplying the band with arms, and ammunition. I must here advert to a trifling incident, to show how hellish was their purpose. With a scarcity of powder, they made many of their recruits, mix it with their brandy; thinking thereby, to excite them more highly. But before their progress was arrested, the practice of drinking had been entirely suppressed.

On Sunday night, the 21st of August, the party mentioned at the dinner, assembled at Mr. Travis' kitchen, and about one or two o'clock, having recovered from their debauch, they commenced their hellish purpose, by applying a ladder to the window, entering it and unbarring the doors. Nat and Hark have the credit of performing the first act. No member of this family ever awoke from their slumbers. With a broadaxe were they all dispatched; and one blow seems to have sufficed for two little boys, who were sleeping so close, that the same stroke nearly severed each neck. Five were murdered at this house; several never changed their positions; but a little infant with its head cut off, was forced to exchange its cradle for the fire-place — Here were obtained several guns, which were deliberately cleaned and loaded; the horses on the plantation saddled, and their career commenced. Proceeding in a zigzag course, they visited every house on their way to Captain Newit Harris'; and no soul escaped them through clemency. In this part of their route, they numbered with the dead a methodist, who had preached, where several of them were present the day before. A division was there effected, for the purpose of extending their devastations, but they soon again united. The last house they visited, before reaching Capt. Harris', was Mr. John T. Barrow's, who although apprised of their intention, could not get away sufficiently soon — overpowered by numbers, he resisted manfully, and the savages who butchered him, paid a trubute to

---

[3]The fortuitous capture of British Major John André exposed the treason of Benedict Arnold during the American Revolution.

his memory, by repeatedly saying "there were no more Tom Barrows to contend with." His wife miraculously escaped, but witnessed the deadly struggle. Arriving at Captain Harris', the family having just escaped, with their numbers increased, they plundered the house, and set off directly for Jerusalem. It was just before they reached the last mentioned house, that I, with a party of volunteers, fell in their route—and pursuing them, we found the blood hardly congealed, in the houses they had left. Within two and a half or three miles of Jerusalem, their progress was arrested—and though pursued the whole night, fortune seemed to sport with us, by bringing us nearer together, and yet, making us pursue separate routes. The families, however, throughout the county, were then placed upon their guard, and no more murders committed. Their last effort at plunder and murder, was made in their attack on Dr. Saml. Blunt's house, where they met with a reception worthy of the gallant little force that gave it. It would be here unjust, not to advert to the determined firmness of Mr. D. W. Fitzhugh, the leader I believe of the little band. And here another circumstance corroborated in a slight degree, my opinion that the insurrection was not general—the slaves of Dr. Blunt, many in number, joined heart and hand in defence of their master. The force of the band was there much broken by desertion; and on that, and the following day, most of them were shot.

In retracing on Tuesday morning the route pursued by the banditti, consisting of a distance of 20 miles, my imagination was struck with more horror, then the most dreadful carnage in a field of battle could have produced. The massacre before me, being principally of helpless women and children. At Levi Waller's the spectacle was truly touching; there, for the first time, I saw at one of those fated houses, a living white soul; and this consisted of a little girl about 12 years of age, looking with an agonized countenance, in a heap of dead bodies lying before her; nine of them women and children; her sister, among the number. She gave me a minute account of the tragedy there acted, having witnessed it from her place of concealment. Congratulating her on having escaped, she said with much simplicity, "that she knew the Lord protected her." I was more affected, and there appeared to my mind, more true religion in that simple remark, from a child, than I have heard a preacher utter in raving an hour. In visiting each house, the mind became sick, and its sensibilities destroyed. Not a single rumor of mercy was heard to break in upon the fiend-like track of these wretches. The slaves through fear having gone to the woods, the houses seemed tenanted only by the dead. The gait the negroes travelled, served to strike additional horror.

For they never rode at less than full speed; and as their horses became tired, they pressed fresh ones. Billy Artis, against whose name there seems a prescription, was conspicuous among the insurgents; when pressed into service, he wept like a child, but having once tasted blood, he was like a wolf let into the fold. Tortured by his conscience, and too proud to surrender, he was his own destroyer. In future years, the bloody road, will give rise to many a sorrowful legend; and the trampling of hoofs, in fancy, visit many an excited imagination.

Below is a correct list of the whites who have been murdered: Joseph Travis, wife and three children; Mrs. Elizabeth Turner, Hartwell Peebles and Sarah Newsome; Mrs. Piety Reese and Son William; Trajan Doyal; Henry Bryant, wife, child and wife's mother; Mrs. Catharine Whitehead, son Richard, four daughters, and grand child; Salatheil Francis; Nathaniel Francis's overseer, and two children; John T. Barrow, and George W. Vaughan; Mrs. Levi Waller and ten children; Wm. Williams, wife and two boys; Mrs. Caswell Worrell and child; Mrs. Rebecca Vaughan, son Arthur, and niece Ann E. Vaughan; Mrs. John R. Williams and child; Mrs. Jacob Williams, and three children; and Edwin Drury, amounting to fifty-five.

I have now hurried through my promised narrative, and feel relieved at quitting so gloomy a subject, but must trespass yet a few moments longer on the patience of the reader. Rumors have no doubt gone abroad, relative to the number of blacks killed; a few remarks on this head, will not then, be deemed improper. From the best evidence which I have been able to obtain, likewise from what I actually saw, the number 40 will include every insurgent who was with them for the least time, throughout their whole route. The fact of their being mounted, and their irregular mode of riding, caused their number to appear much greater than it really was. Our Court has manifested great clemency in listening with unwearied patience to the examination of a multitude of witnesses, and to long and elaborate arguments of counsel. And their judgments reflect credit upon our county, when it is remarked, that there is not an individual who disapproves of one of their convictions. They have condemned to death one and twenty persons. Thirteen have been executed, a commutation of punishment in several cases recommended, and there are something like five and twenty prisoners yet to be tried. A commutation in several cases I have warmly supported, and here add my approbation of the course pursued by the court when the testimony seemed to call for it. Those who have been condemned to death and those actually shot, exceed the number attributed to the insurgents.

It follows then, as a necessary consequence, that several innocent persons must have suffered. For those who have been bereft of their relations, by this unfortunate occurrence, many allowances are to be made: but to another class, who have not even this plea for shedding the blood of the innocent, should not the violated laws of their country call them to a settlement? They must bear in mind that the matter has one day to be adjudicated before an impartial judge. Scarcely a mail arrives that does not bring some account of an isolated conviction for insurrection in remote counties—thus Spottsylvania, Nansemond, Prince George, &c. Should the views here taken by me, prove that the insurrection was not a general one, and thereby save the life of a human being, I shall be more than compensated for the time consumed, together with the odium called down upon me, by the expression of *my opinions.* In remote counties, I cannot conceive how an isolated conviction can take place for insurrection, unless the Court believe the prisoner to have had some knowledge of the affair here. I have no doubt but that many superstitious remarks made by the slaves, on the consequences of the singular appearance of the sun, unconnected in their minds with any other subject, have been construed into a knowledge of insurrection. Likewise, if mere declarations made by slaves, relative to what they would do if *Captain Nat* came that way, the insurrection, being at that time suppressed, *Nat's* party dispersed, and most of them shot, are to be construed into evidences of guilt, there can be no end to convictions. The excitement having now subsided, which induced many to think wrong, and prevented many who thought right from stemming the tide, it becomes us as men to return to our duty. Without manifesting a fear of the blacks, by keeping a stationed armed force in any section of our country, let us adopt a more efficient plan, by keeping up for some time, a regular patrol, always under the command of a discreet person, who will not by indiscriminate punishment, goad these miserable wretches into a state of desperation.

8

The Norfolk Herald

November 4, 1831

This account details the capture of Nat Turner by local resident Benjamin Phipps.

Nat Turner Certainly Taken!

We were . . . politely favored with the perusal of a letter from Southampton, to a gentlemen in this place, from which we are enabled to give the following statement, corroborating the one published in our last, with some interesting additions:

Nat was shot at by Mr. Francis, (as stated in our last) on Thursday, (yesterday week,) near a fodder stack in his field, but happening to fall at the moment of the discharge, the contents of the pistol passed through the crown of his hat. He had the hat on his head when he was taken, with the shot holes in it, which he exhibited to shew how narrowly he had escaped being shot. . . .

He was taken about a mile and a half from the house of Mr. Travis, the man he served, and whose family, including himself, were the first victims of this cruel fanatic and his besotted followers. He had made himself a sort of den in the lap of a fallen tree, which he had covered over with pine brush. His head was protruded through this covering, as if he was in the act of reconnoitering, when Mr. Phipps, (who had that morning, for the first time, turned out in pursuit of him) came suddenly upon him. Mr. Phipps not knowing him, demanded "Who are you?" and was answered, "*I am Nat Turner.*" Mr. Phipps then ordered him to hand out his arms, and he delivered up a sword, which was the only weapon he had.

Mr. Phipps then took him to Mr. Edwards', whence the news of his capture spread so rapidly, that in less than an hour a hundred persons had collected at the place, whose feelings on beholding the blood-stained monster, were so much excited, that it was with difficulty he could be conveyed alive to Jerusalem.

The Norfolk Herald, Norfolk, Virginia, November 4, 1831.

He is said to be very free in his confessions, which, however, are no further important than as shewing that he was instigated by the wildest superstition and fanaticism, and was not connected with any organized plan of conspiracy beyond the circle of the few ignorant wretches whom he had seduced by his artifices to join him. He still pretends that he is a prophet, and relates a number of revelations which he says he has had, from which he was induced to believe that he could succeed in conquoring *the county of Southampton!* (what miserable ignorance!) as the white people did in the revolution.

He says the idea of an insurrection never crossed his mind until a few months before he started with it; and he considered *the dark appearance of the sun* as a signal for him to commence! His profanity in comparing his pretended prophecies with passages in the Holy Scriptures should not be mentioned, if it did not afford proof of his insanity. Yet it was by that means he obtained the complete control of his followers, which led them to the perpetration of the horrible deeds of the 22d August.

9

The Norfolk Herald
November 14, 1831

This article was republished in The Richmond Enquirer *of November 18, 1831. It offers a rare contemporary account of Nat Turner's death.*

NAT TURNER.—This wretched culprit expiated his crimes (crimes at the bare mention of which the blood runs cold) on Friday last. He betrayed no emotion, but appeared to be utterly reckless in the awful fate that awaited him, and even hurried the executioner in the performance of his duty!—Precisely at 12 o'clock he was launched into eternity—There were but a few people to see him hanged—[. . . *appropos* the Albany biographer of Negro cut-throats will please to remember, that Nat was not torn limbless by horses, but simply "hanged by the neck until he was dead." — He may say, however, that *General* Nat sold his body for dissection, and spent the money in ginger cakes.]

A gentleman of Jerusalem has taken down his confession, which he intends to publish with an accurate likeness of the brigand, taken by Mr. John Crowley, portrait painter of this town, to be lithographed by *Endicott & Swett*, of Baltimore.

10

Excerpts from the Court Records of Southampton County

1831

The trials of the forty-nine men and one woman accused of participation in the Nat Turner rebellion occurred over a period of nearly three months, from August 31 to November 21, 1831. They took place in the Southampton Court of Oyer and Terminer, a county-level court authorized to conduct trials of enslaved people in capital cases. Most trials were held before a group of five justices of the peace, although this number expanded to ten for the trial of Nat Turner. Virginia governor John Floyd was particularly concerned that the rebellion trials should be conducted in the fairest manner possible. To monitor the tribunal, he directed the court to send him a verbatim transcript of each proceeding. Unfortunately, although the court complied with the governor's request for copies of its trial records, it created and supplied case summaries rather than verbatim transcripts.

The trial records reproduced here are excerpted from The Southampton County Minute Book, 1830–1835, *preserved on microfilm at the Virginia State Library, Archives Branch. They are presented with only minor editorial changes. The original records include no headings indicating the name of the person being tried. I have added these for clarity. Where the original record includes words that had been crossed out, I have deleted these words from this version; and where additions*

The Southampton County Minute Book, 1830–1835, Virginia State Library, Archives Branch.

have been interlineated, I have written them into the text. I have also deleted marginal notes that indicate that the transcript had been copied and sent to the governor. Otherwise the document is an exact copy of the original version—retaining all the ambiguity and confused wording of the original.

Trial of Daniel

Present: Jeremiah Cobb, James D. Massenburg, Meriwether P. Peete, James Trezevant and Ores Browne—Gent Justices.

Meriwether B. Broadnax, attorney for the Commonwealth filed an Information[1] against the prisoners above named. And thereupon Daniela negro man slave the property of Richard Porter on the said Information mentioned was brought into Court and set to the Bar in custody of the Jailor of this county and the Court doth assign William C. Parker, Esq., Atty. to defend the prisoner and as the prisoner being duly arraigned · of the premises pleaded not guilty to the Information and Levi Waller a witness on behalf of the Commonwealth was sworn and disposed[2] as follows. That on Monday the 22d August 1831 a number of negroes, say between 40 and 50, came to the house of the witness mounted on horseback and armed with guns and swords and other weapons—the witness and all his family attempted to make their escape and the witness did make his escape but did not proceed far from his house before he hid himself in sight of the house where he could see nearly all things that · transpired at the house—That the witness saw the prisoner Daniel & two other negroes named Aaron and Sam go into a log house where the witnesses wife and a small girl had attempted to secrete themselves—he saw the negroes come out of the house and the prisoner Daniel had the witnesses' wife's [word blurred] chain in his hand—the witness then made for a swamp further from the house and was pursued by two of the negroes but they did not overtake him. [A]fter the negroes had left the witnesses house the witness returned to the house · and found his wife and the small girl as well as many other members of his family murdered and an infant child mortally wounded who died the Wednesday evening following.

[1]Complaint or charge.
[2]Probably a misspelling of "deposed."

Nathaniel Francis also a witness for the Commonwealth was sworn and deposed to the following facts—that a number, say between 50 and 60 free white persons were murdered on Sunday night the 21st & Monday morning the 22d day of August 1831 by a number of negroes and it was generally believed that there was insurrection among the negroes of this County.

Sampson C. Reese also a witness for the Commonwealth being sworn says that he was in company with a number of other gentlemen and in pursuit of a company of negroes who were from report in a State of insurrection in this County—that they came up with the insurgents at Mr. James W. Parkers—the first negro he saw after getting to Mr. Parkers gate was the prisoner at the bar on Dr. Musgraves horse—the witness shot at the prisoner—the prisoner had no arms that the witness saw.

Richard Porter a witness on behalf of the prisoner being sworn says he was told the prisoner had surrendered himself and was going to his the witness house and the prisoner was at home Monday morning—he saw nothing uncommon about the prisoner. The court after hearing the testimony and on due consideration thereof are unanimously of opinion that the prisoner is guilty in manner and form as in the information against him is set forth and it being demanded of him if anything for himself he had or knew to say why the court should not proceed to pronounce judgment against him and nothing being offered or alleged in delay of judgment it is considered by the Court that the prisoner be hanged by the neck until he be dead and that execution of this judgment be done upon him the said Daniel by the Sheriff of this County on Monday the 5th day of September next between the hours of ten o'clock in the forenoon and two o'clock in the afternoon of the same day at the usual place of execution. And thereupon the prisoner is remanded to Jail. Memo: The Court values the said slave Daniel to the sum of one hundred dollars. Absent Jeremiah Cobb & Alex P. Peete. Present Robert Goodwin and James W. Parker Gent.

Trial of Tom

Tom late the property of Caty Whitehead named in the said information was then set to the bar in custody of the Jailor of this Court and being arraigned of the premises pleaded not guilty to the information and James L. French Esq. attorney at Law is by the Court appointed to defend the prisoner. And thereupon the Court after hearing the testimony are of opinion and doth accordingly order that the said Tom be discharged from further prosecution for this said supposed offense.

Trial of Jack

Present. Carr Bowers, James D. Masserburg, James W. Parker, James Trezevant and Ores A. Browne, Gent. Justices.

Jack a negro slave late the property of Caty Whitehead who hath been heretofore arraigned and pleaded not guilty to the information filed against the said Jack and others was again led to the bar in custody of the Jailor of this County and Venus a negro slave was sworn charged and examined as a witness for the Commonwealth and deposes as follows. That the prisoner Jack with one other slave of Mrs. Whitehead named Andrew came to the witness masters house Mr. Richard Porter on Monday before the last at about 9 o'clock in the morning and said all the white people were killed and inquired if the negroes had killed their white people there, she told them they had not for they were gone before the negroes got there. They then enquired where the black people were (meaning the negroes that had been there, and were in insurrection). She told them they had gone, the prisoner and Andrew said they were going on after them, that the negroes had left word for them to go on after them and they did not know what else to do, and they went off, the witness understood that the prisoner and Andrew were going to join the insurgents they were both on one horse.

Hubbard a slave being charged and sworn says the negroes came to his mistress and murdered her and family that the prisoner and two other negroes belonging to his mistress went from home, after some time the prisoner & Andrew returned and asked if the negroes were gone and the prisoner and Andrew caught a horse and rode off. The Witness thought they went to join the insurgents. The prisoner appeared to be much disturbed.

Wallace a negro slave being charged and sworn as a witness on behalf of the prisoner states that he was at home at the house of his mistress Mrs. Caty Whitehead when a band of insurgent negroes rode up. Jack and Andrew ran off before any murder was committed—went off and returned several hours after and said they had been to Mr. Booths and Mr. Powells, the prisoner and Andrew appeared much distressed greatly grieved but took a horse and rode off. Thomas Hathcock a free man of colour being charged and sworn as a witness for the prisoner—says the prisoner and Andrew came to his house, asked what they should do, much grieved—went with him to several houses George Booth also a witness for the prisoner being sworn says that the prisoner and Andrew came to his house, told him of the massacre and said "Lord have mercy upon them for they know not what to do—" James Powell also a witness for the prisoner being sworn says he found the prisoner and Andrew at his house, they came when called very humble and much grieved—they went with him to the Cross Keys and were there taken in custody.

The Court after hearing the testimony and the prisoner by James T. French Esq assigned counsel for the prisoner in his defense are unanimously of opinion that the prisoner is guilty in manner and form as in the information against him is set forth and it being demanded of the prisoner if anything for himself he had or knew to say why the Court should not proceed to pronounce judgment against him and nothing being offered or alleged in delay of Judgment it is considered by the Court that the prisoner be taken hence to the place from whence he came there to be safely kept until Monday the twelfth day of September instant on which day between the hours of nine o'clock in the forenoon and two o'clock in the afternoon the prisoner is to be taken by the Sheriff to the usual place of execution and there be hanged by the neck until he is dead. And the court values the said Jack to the sum of four hundred and fifty dollars—and the Court for sufficient reasons appearing doth recommend to the Governor to commute the punishment of the prisoner—

Trial of Andrew

Andrew a negro slave late the property of Caty Whitehead was set to the bar in custody of the Jailor of this County and being arraigned pleaded not guilty to the information and Venus a negro slave was charged and sworn to witness on behalf of the Commonwealth says that the prisoner and Jack a slave of Mrs. Whitehead came to her master's, Richard Porter's, house on the Monday before the last about 9 o'clock in the morning and said all the white people were killed and enquired if the negroes had killed the white people there, she told them they had not for they were gone before the negroes got there, they then enquired where the black people were—(meaning the negroes that had been there and were in insurrection.) She told them they were gone. The prisoner and Jack said they were going on after them, that the negroes had left word for them to go on after them and they did not know what else to do and they went off and the witness understood that the prisoner and Jack were going to join the insurgents—they were on one horse.

Hubbard a slave was charged and sworn—says that the negroes came to his mistresses and murdered her and family—that the prisoner and two other negroes belonging to his mistress went from home, after sometime the prisoner and Jack returned and asked if the *negroes* were gone. And the prisoner and Jack caught a horse and rode off, the witness thought they went off to join the insurgents, the prisoner appeared to be much distressed. Whereupon the Court after hearing the testimony and the prisoner by James L. French his counsel assigned him by the Court in his defense are unanimously of opinion that the prisoner is guilty in manner and form as in the information against him as set forth, and it being demanded of the prisoner if anything for himself he had or knew to say why the Court should not proceed to pronounce judgment against him according to law and nothing being offered or alleged in delay of Judgment it is considered by the Court that the prisoner be taken hence to the place from whence he came there to be safely kept until Monday the twelfth day of September Instant on which day between the hours of ten o'clock in the forenoon and two o'clock in the afternoon the prisoner is to be taken by the Sheriff to the usual place of execution, and there to be hanged by the neck until he be dead. And the Court doth value the said slave Andrew to the sum of four hundred dollars. And the Court for sufficient reasons shown doth recommend to the Governor to commute the punishment of the prisoner.

Trials of Nathan, Tom, and Davy

At a Court of Oyer and Terminer continued by adjournment and held for the County of Southampton on the 6th day of September 1831 for the trial of Nathan a negro man slave belonging to the estate of Benjamin Blunt, dcsd.[3] & Nathan, Tom, and Davy, negro boy slaves belonging to Nathaniel Francis, charged with consulting, advising and conspiring with divers other slaves to rebel and make insurrection and making insurrection and plotting to take the lives of divers free white persons citizens of this Commonwealth.

Present: William B. Goodwyn, James W. Parker, James Trezevant, Alexander P. Peete & Joseph T. Claud. Gent.

The Court being thus constituted M. B. Broadnax Atty. for the Commonwealth filed an Information against the prisoner & the prisoner Nathan the property of the Estate of Benjamin Blunt dcsd. was set to the bar in custody of the Jailor of this County and the Court doth assign James L. French Esq. Counsel for the prisoner in his defense and the said Nathan being arraigned of the premises pleaded not guilty to the information and Daniel a negro boy slave being sworn and charged as a witness for the Commonwealth says [that] he was confined in the jail

---

[3]Deceased.

of Greensville County as a runaway at the time the prisoner was also confined in said jail, that the prisoner said he had been present when the murders had been committed by the insurgents—the prisoner had blood on his breeches which he said he had told the white people was cider. Moses a negro boy slave was sworn and charged as a witness for the prisoner and says that the prisoner went unwillingly—that he committed no murder and he thinks had no opportunity to escape and remained with the negroes till they dispersed.

The Court after hearing the testimony and from all the circumstances of the case are unanimously of opinion that the prisoner is guilty in manner and form as in the information against them is set forth and it being demanded of the prisoner if anything for himself he had or knew to say why the Court should not proceed to pronounce judgment against him according to Law and nothing being offered or alleged in delay of judgment it is considered by the Court that the prisoner be taken hence to the jail from which he was taken therein to be safely confined until Monday the twelfth day of September instant on which day between the hours of ten o'clock in the morning and two o'clock in the afternoon the prisoner is to be taken by the Sheriff to the usual place of execution and there be hanged by the neck until he be dead. And the Court values the said slave Nathan to the sum of three hundred and seventy five dollars.

Nathan, Tom and Davy negro boy slaves the property of Nathl. Francis were then set to the bar in custody of the jailor of this County and being arraigned of the premises pleaded not guilty to the information. Thomas R. Gray, William C. Parker and James L. French being assigned by the Court Counsel for the prisoners and [paragraph abruptly ends here].

Moses a negro boy slave being charged and sworn as a witness for the Commonwealth says that the three prisoners were taken from Nathl. Francis and placed one behind each of the company that they went unwillingly but continued with them the whole of Monday—witnessed many of the murders but were constantly guarded by negroes with guns who were ordered to shoot them if they attempted to escape. They remained until the whole troop were dispersed. [Q]uestion being asked by the Court relative to the ages of the prisoners it appeared that the oldest was not more than 15 years, the other two much younger, the oldest very badly grown.

The Court after hearing the testimony and all the circumstances of the case are unanimously of opinion that the prisoners are guilty in manner and form as in the information against them is set forth and it being demanded of each of them if anything for themselves they have or know to say why the Court should not proceed to pronounce judgment against them according to Law and nothing being offered or alleged in delay of judgment it is considered by the Court that the prisoners be taken hence to the jail from which they were taken therein to be safely confined until Tuesday the 20th day of September instant on which day between the hours of ten o'clock in the morning and two o'clock in the afternoon they be taken by the Sheriff to the usual place of execution and there to be hanged by the neck until each of them be dead and the Court from all the circumstances of the case do recommend to the Governor to commute the punishment of the said Nathan, Tom and Davy to transportation. And the Court doth value the said slaves to the sum of three hundred dollars each.

The Court doth allow James L. French the sum of ten dollars his fee for defending Nathan a slave the property of the estate of Benjamin Blunt and to James L. French, William C. Parker & Thomas R. Gray the sum of ten dollars each for defending Nathan, Tom and Davy negro slaves belonging to Nathaniel Francis. It having been intimated to the Court that the military force assembled at this place will be discharged in a few days the Court believing that a strong guard is necessary to the safe keeping of the prisoners now in jail until such as are condemned may be executed respectfully solicit General Eppes the Commanding Officer to retain at this place fifty men as a guard for the jail and the Clerk of this Court is directed to deliver to General Eppes a copy of this order.

WM. B. GOODWYN

Trial of Lucy

Lucy a negro woman slave late the property of John T. Barrow who stands charged with conspiring to rebel and make insurrection was this day set to the bar in custody of the jailor of this County (the Court summoned for her trial having failed to meet) and the Court doth assign Wm. C. Parker Counsel for the prisoner in her defense and Meriwether B. Broadnax atty. prosecuting for the Commonwealth filed an Information against the said Lucy and thereupon the said Lucy being arraigned of the premises pleaded not guilty to the information—and [original text missing]

Mary T. Barrow a witness for the Commonwealth being sworn says that on the 22d of Aug. last when the insurgents came to the house of her late husband, John T. Barrow, and were entering the yard and she the witness was making her escape the prisoner a girl about 20 years of age seized and held her about one minute and until another negro took her away—that she does not know certainly what her intentions were but thought it was to detain her. Bird a negro slave being charged and sworn as a witness for the Commonwealth says that he found several weeks after the murder of Mr. Barrow four pieces of money in a bag of feathers and covered with a handkerchief—that the room was occupied by the prisoner and another (Moses since hung). Moses a slave was sworn and charged as a witness for the Commonwealth & says that after the murder was committed he saw the prisoner in company with the insurgents at the door. Robert T. Musgrave being sworn as a witness for the Commonwealth says that after his examining the prisoner she stated that she had fled through the kitchen and concealed herself in the cornfield—The Court after hearing the testimony and from all the circumstances of the case are unanimously of opinion that the prisoner is guilty in manner and form as in the information against her is set forth and it being demanded of the prisoner if anything for herself she had or knew to say why the Court should not proceede to pronounce judgment against her according to Law & nothing being offered or alleged in delay of judgment it is considered by the Court that the prisoner be taken hence to the jail from whence she was taken therein to be safely confined until Monday the 26th of September instant on which day between the hours of ten o'clock in the forenoon and two o'clock in the afternoon the prisoner is to be taken by the Sheriff to the usual place of execution and there be hanged by the neck until she be dead. And the Court value the said Lucy to the sum of Two hundred and Seventy five dollars.

Trial of Jack

Jack a negro man slave the property of Everett Bryant was this day set to the bar in custody of the Jailor of this County (the Court summoned for his trial having failed to meet) charged with conspiring to rebel and make insurrection, and Meriwether B. Broadnax Attorney for the Commonwealth filed an information against the prisoner and the Court doth assign William C. Parker Counsel for the prisoner in his defense and the prisoner being arraigned of the premises pleaded not guilty to the information. The Court after hearing the testimony and from all the circumstances are of the opinion that the prisoner is not guilty as in pleading he hath alleged and proclamation being made as the manner is and nothing further appearing or being alleged against the prisoner it is ordered that the prisoner be forthwith discharged from custody—Absent—William B. Goodwyn & Joseph T. Claude & Alex. P. Peet. Present James W. Parker, James Trezevant—Gent & Ores A. Browne—Gent.

Trials of Jim, Isaac, and Preston

At a Court of Oyer and Terminer continued by adjournment and held for the County of Southampton on the 22d day of September 1831 for the trial of Jim and Isaac negro men slaves the property of Samuel Champion and Preston a negro man slave the property of Hannah Williamson charged with conspiring to rebel and making insurrection.

Present—James W. Parker, Jacob Barnes, James Trezevant, Ores A. Browne and Alexander Myrick. Gent.

The Court being thus constituted Meriwether B. Broadnax Attorney prosecuting for the Commonwealth filed an Information against the said Jim, Isaac & Preston & thereupon the said Jim and Isaac were set to the bar in custody of the Jailor of this County and being arraigned of the premises pleaded not guilty to the information and Beck a slave being charged and sworn as a witness for the Commonwealth says that on the 15th day of August last at a black persons house at Solomon Parkers she heard the prisoners say that if the black people came they would join and help kill the white people it was after they had been talking some time that she went in and did not hear the Commencement of the conversation there were several slaves present and one of them stated that his master had crossed him and he would be crossed before the end of the year. Witness had heard three other slaves make use of the same declaration some time previously in the neighborhood—prisoners lived about a mile from Solomon Parkers. They told her it was a secret and if she told the white persons would shoot her—Witness's mistress went to Sussex upon the alarm of the late insurrection and while there witness's mistress said she wondered if her negroes were concerned upon which witness made the above statement in substance. Witness states that the reason of her not telling before was that she did not understand it. States that Jim denied he knew the witness on his examination before the Magistrate in Sussex—Witness states that she is a house servant and is seldom in the outhouses—[4]

Bob a slave being sworn and charged as a witness for the Commonwealth says that the Monday night of the insurrection Isaac one of the prisoners left home and on his return stated he had been to Solomon Parkers and on Monday night before after the August meeting both

---

[4]The quarters for enslaved people.

prisoners went to Solomon Parkers—Witness states that Jim frequently went to Solomon Parkers—And the prisoners were fully heard in their defense by James L. French their Counsel the Court after hearing the testimony and from all the circumstances of the case are unanimously of opinion that the prisoners are guilty in manner and form as in the information against them is set forth and it being demanded of each of them if anything for themselves they have or knew to say why the Court should not proceed to pronounce Judgment against them according to Law and nothing being offered or alleged in delay of judgment it is considered by the Court that the prisoners be taken hence to the jail from whence they came therein to be safely confined until Friday the 30th day of September instant, on which day between the hours of ten o'clock in the forenoon and four o'clock in the afternoon they are to be taken by the Sheriff of this County to the usual place of execution & there be hanged by the neck until each of them be dead. And the Court value the said slave Jim to the sum of three hundred dollars and the said slave Isaac to the sum of four hundred dollars—

11

Nat Turner's Trial Record

Excerpt from the Court Records of Southampton County

1831

Nat Turner eluded capture for over two months. But once he was in custody, the justice system moved swiftly. He was apprehended on October 30, tried on November 5, and hanged on November 11.

At a Court of Oyer and Terminer summoned and held for the County of Southampton on Saturday the fifth day of November 1831 for the trial of Nat alias Nat Turner a negro man slave the property of Putnam Moore an infant charged with conspiring to rebel and making insurrection—

The Southampton County Minute Book, 1830–1835, Virginia State Library, Archives Branch.

Present—Jeremiah Cobb, Samuel B. Hines, James D. Massenburg, James W. Parker, Robert Goodwin, James Trezevant & Ores A. Browne— Gent. Carr Bowers, Thomas Preston and Richd A. Urquardt.

For reasons appearing to the Court it is ordered that the Sheriff summon a sufficient additional guard to repel any attempt that may be made to remove Nat alias Nat Turner from the custody of the Sheriff—

The prisoner Nat alias Nat Turner was set to the bar in custody of the Jailor of this County, and William C. Parker is by the Court assigned Counsel for the prisoner in his defense, and Meriwether B. Broadnax attorney for the Commonwealth filed an Information against the prisoner who upon his arraignment pleaded not guilty and Levi Waller being summoned as a Witness states that on the morning of the 22d day of August last between 9 and 10 o'clock he heard that the negroes had risen and were murdering the whites and were coming. Witness sent his son Thos. to the school house he living about a quarter of a mile off to let it be known & for his children to come home. Mr. Crocker the School Master came with the Witnesses children Witness told him to go to the house and load the guns, but before the guns were loaded Mr. Crocker came to the still where witness was—and said they were in Sight. Witness retreated and concealed himself in the corner of the fence in the weeds behind the garden on the opposite side of the house. Several negroes pursued him but he escaped them by falling among the weeds over the fence—One negro rode up and looked over, but did not observe him—The attention of the party he thinks were called off from him by some of the party going in pursuit of another, which he thinks they took for him but who turned out to be his blacksmith—Witness then retreated into the swamp which was not far off—After remaining some time witness again approached the house—before he retreated he saw several of his family murdered by the negroes—Witness crept up near the house to see what they were doing and concealed himself by getting in the plumb orchard behind the garden the negroes were drinking—Witness saw prisoner whom he knew very well, mounted (he thought on Dr. Musgrave's horse) stated that the prisoner seemed to command the party—made Peter Edwards' negro man Sam who seemed disposed to remain mount his horse and go with them—prisoner gave command to the party to "go ahead" when they left his house—Witness states that he cannot be mistaken in the identity of the prisoner—James Trezevant being sworn said that Mr. James W. Parker and himself were the Justices before whom the prisoner was examined prior to his commitment—That the prisoner at the time was in confinement but no threats or promises were held out to him to make any disclosures. That he admitted he was one of the insurgents engaged in the late insurrection, and the Chief among them—that he gave to his master and mistress Mr. Travis and his wife the first blow before they were dispatched that he killed Miss Peggy Whitehead—that he was with the insurgents from their first movement to their dispersion on the Tuesday morning after the insurrection took place—That he gave a long account of the motives which lead him finally to commence the bloody scenes which took place—That he pretended to have had intimations by signed omens from God that he should embark in the desperate attempt—That his comrades and even he were impressed with a belief that he could by the imposition of his hands cure disease—That he related a particular instance in which it was believed that he had in that manner effected a cure upon one of his comrades, and that he went on to detail a medley of incoherent and confused opinions about his communications with God, his command over the clouds etc., etc. which he had been entertaining as far back as 1826.

The Court after hearing the testimony and from all the circumstances of the case are unanimously of opinion that the prisoner is guilty in manner and form as in the Information against him alleged, and it being demanded of him if anything for himself he had or knew to say by the Court to judgment and execution against him of and upon the premises should not procede—he said he had nothing but what he had before said. Therefore it is considered by the Court that he be taken hence to the Jail from whence he was taken therein to remain until Friday the 11th day of November instant, on which day between the hours of ten o'clock in the forenoon and four o'clock in the afternoon he is to be taken by the Sheriff to the usual place of execution and then and there be hanged by the neck until he be dead. And the Court value the said slave to the sum of three hundred and seventy five dollars.

Ordered that William C. Parker be allowed the sum of ten dollars as a fee for defending Nat alias Nat Turner, late the property of Putnam Moore, an infant.

JMH. COBB

12

Excerpts from the Diary of Virginia Governor John Floyd
1831–1832

Governor John Floyd was forty-eight years old at the time of the Nat Turner rebellion. He began his political career during the War of 1812 with election to the Virginia House of Delegates. He was then elected to the U.S. House of Representatives in 1817 and to the office of governor in 1829. His handling of the Nat Turner rebellion and its aftermath was the most important act of his years in government service.

Floyd's diary catalogs his military and political response to the Nat Turner insurrection. He describes the orders he gave dispatching militia units and arms to Southampton County and to other counties that were fearful of insurrection. The diary also indicates that he closely followed the trials of the rebels and that, based on the recommendation of the Southampton County Court, he commuted many sentences to transportation and sale out of the state. After the rebellion, Floyd supported the political forces in Virginia favoring gradual emancipation. However, it seems clear from sources external to the diary that the governor understood the volatile nature of such a position, and at the last minute he retreated from assuming a central leadership role on this issue. He backed away from openly advocating emancipation in his December 6, 1831, message to the legislature. Hence, the initiative passed into the hands of members of the House of Delegates.

August 1831

Twenty-third day. This will be a very noted day in Virginia. At daylight this morning the Mayor of the City put into my hands a notice to the public, written by James Trezvant of Southampton County, stating that an insurrection of the slaves in that county had taken place, that several families had been massacred and that it would take a considerable military force to put them down.

The diary entries presented here are excerpted from Charles H. Ambler, *The Life and Diary of John Floyd* (Richmond, Va.: Richmond Press, 1918).

Upon the receipt of this information, I began to consider how to prepare for the crisis. To call out the militia and equip a military force for that service. But according to the forms of this wretched and abominable Constitution, I must first require advice of Council, and then disregard it, if I please. On this occasion there was not one councillor in the city. I went on, made all the arrangements for suppressing the insurrection, having all my orders ready for men, arms, ammunition, etc., when by this time, one of the council came to town, and that vain and foolish ceremony was gone through. In a few hours the troops marched, Captain Randolph with a fine troop of cavalry and Captain John B. Richardson with light artillery, both from this city and two companies of Infantry from Norfolk and Portsmouth. The light Artillery had under their care one thousand stand of arms for Southampton and Sussex, with a good supply of ammunition. All these things were dispatched in a few hours.

Twenty-fourth day. This day was spent in distributing arms below this where it was supposed it would be wanted.

Twenty-fifth day. I received dispatches from Brigadier Richard Eppes, stating with local militia those I sent him were more than enough to suppress the insurrection.

Twenty-sixth day. Constant application for arms are made. I received letters from W. O. Goode of Mecklenburg and James H. Gholson for arms. They were sent. General Eppes disbanded the Artillery and Infantry who returned home.

Twenty-seventh day. I received from Brigadier-General Broadnax a letter giving an account of his having assumed command of Brunswick and of the insurrection at Hick's Ford in Greenville.

Twenty-eighth day. General Broadnax disbanded those troops and returned home. He reports several families killed the same day dispatches were received from General Eppes stating the names of many who were killed. From the two accounts, I find that there have been murdered by the negro insurgents sixty-one persons! The accounts received from the seat of war informs me that the operation of the troops is now confined to the capturing of the insurgents as they can make no further resistance and are endeavoring to escape.

Twenty-ninth day. The news heretofore from below, Surry and Nansemond, is in expectation of an insurrection. The Commandants of those regiments ask for arms. They are sent them.

A few days ago the mayor of Fredericksburg and the Colonel of that regiment informed me that the negroes there have been detected in a conspiracy, and desired arms. They have been sent them.

Thirtieth day. The news as heretofore. General Thomas captured most of the insurgents. The principal leaders yet untaken. Nat, alias Nat Turner, by the negroes called General, heretofore a preacher and a slave, Artis and some others are yet sought.

Thirty-first day. I learn that many negroes have been taken up in the county of Nansemond, about forty, some of whom inform us of its being intended as a general rising of the negroes.

September 1831

First day. General Eppes informed me that they had captured about forty of the insurgents, that they have been confined in the Southampton jail and have been turned over to the courts of that County to be dealt with according to law.

Second day. The same information as yesterday.

Third day. General Eppes informs me by the return of Captain Harrison of the Cavalry, whose troops returned to-day, that a Court of Oyer and Terminer for Southampton County was convened on the thirty-first of August and continued the first of September and had convicted some of the prisoners of conspiracy and murder.

A few hours after this he sent an express with the record of the court, containing the trial and condemnation of four of the prisoners, Moses and Daniel, Andrew and Jack. The last two the court recommended their punishment to be commuted for transportation, to which I will agree. Moses and David will be hanged on Monday, the fifth. Throughout this affair the most appalling accounts have been given of the conduct of the negroes, the most inhuman butcheries the mind can conceive of, men, women, and infants, their heads chopped off, their bowels ripped out, ears, noses, hands, and legs cut off, no instance of mercy shown. The white people shot them in self defense whenever they appeared.

But amidst these scenes there were slaves found to defend their masters and to give information of the approach of the hostile party. These insurgents progressed twenty miles before they were checked, yet all this horrid work was accomplished in two days.

Fourth day. I have written General Eppes to retain at Southampton a sufficient guard and to disband the rest of his forces.

Fifth day. I have received to-day by express a record of the trial of the other slaves, eight of them, concerned in the massacre of Southampton. They are all condemned to be executed on Friday and next Monday. I will not in these cases interfere with the operations of the law. . . .

Seventh day. I am this day informed by a letter from Colonel Wm. A. Christian, Commandant of the twenty-seventh Regiment in Northampton, that the negroes in that county are in a state of insubordination and intend to create an insurrection in that county. Guns have been found among them and some they were compelled to take from them by force. That county and Accomack are well armed, I have sent them a good supply of ammunition by this day's boat. I fear much this insurrection in Southampton is to lead to much more disastrous consequences than is at this time apprehended by anybody. . . .

Ninth day. No news from Southampton though even Prince William County has its emissaries in it from among the free negroes of the District of Columbia. He is a Preacher. The whole of that massacre in Southampton is the work of these Preachers as daily intelligence informs me. I am still unwell.

Tenth day. I received by express to-day the record of the trial of nine others of the slaves concerned in the insurrection of Southampton. Five of these slaves the court recommended to transportation which the law calls commuting this punishment. I am so unwell this afternoon that I have to go to bed. . . .

Fourteenth day. Attended various Boards *ex officio.* This day the record of the trial of Misek, a negro in Greensville, for Conspiracy was brought. The evidence was too feeble and therefore I have reprieved him for sale and transportation.

Sixteenth day. I had a Council of State, transacted business and received the record of nine slaves condemned to be hanged by the Court of Sussex. One I have reprieved. No news from any other part of the State. . . .

Twenty-third day. I received the record of the trial of Lucy and Joe of Southampton. They were of the insurgents. What can be done, I yet know not, as I am obliged by the Constitution first to require the advice of the Council, then I do as I please. This endangers the lives of these negroes, though I am disposed to reprieve for transportation I cannot do it until I first require advice of the Council and there are no councillors now in Richmond, nor will there be unless Daniel comes to town in time enough.

Twenty-sixth day. I have been busily employed sending off arms to distant counties this morning, but the rain put a stop to that operation.

Twenty-seventh day. I have received a record of the trial of three slaves, for treason in Southampton. Am recommended to mercy, which I would grant but the forms of our infamous Constitution makes it necessary before the Governor does any act involving discretionary power, first to require advice of Council, and in this case I cannot do so, because there is not one member of the Council of State in Richmond, wherefore the poor wretch must lose his life by their absence from their official duty.

I have received this day another number of the "Liberator," a newspaper printed in Boston, with the express intention of inciting the slaves and free negroes in this and the other States to rebellion and to murder the men, women and children of those states. Yet we are gravely told there is no law to punish such an offence. The amount of it then is this, a man in our States may plot treason in one state against another without fear of punishment, whilst the suffering state has no right to resist by the provisions of the Federal Constitution. If this is not checked it must lead to a separation of these states. If the forms of law will not punish, the law of nature will not permit men to have their families butchered before their eyes by their slaves and not seek by force to punish those who plan and encourage them to perpetrate these deeds. I shall notice this in my next message to the General Assembly of this State. Something must be done and with decision.

Twenty-ninth day. No councillors in Richmond.

December 1831

Second day. I am busy with my message. Some of my friends to whom I have shown it are afraid it is too bold and strong for the times. I think it right and know it honest, therefore I will send it forth, though it may not suit the palate of the Federal Executive.[1] What is he to me, when the good of the country requires this weak and wicked administration to be stopped in its downward career. . . .

Sixth day. My message was well received, though many think it a bold state paper. It may be their attachment to Jackson has blunted their patriotism. I think so. But it is the true doctrine of the Federal Constitution and States Rights. I will maintain it as long as I am Governor even to the utmost hazard. . . .

Twenty-third day. Letters from the South inform me that my message is still well considered and has much increased my standing and popularity there.

---

[1]This is a reference to Governor Floyd's position in opposition to President Andrew Jackson and in support of South Carolina's nullification of a federal tariff law.

Twenty-sixth day. The public business gets on slowly. The question of the gradual abolition of slavery begins to be mooted. The Eastern members, meaning those east of the Blue Ridge Mountains, wish to avoid the discussion, but it must come if I can influence my friends in the Assembly to bring it on. I will not rest until slavery is abolished in Virginia.

January 1832

Ninth day. Members begin to talk of debating the question of gradually emancipating the Slaves of Virginia. It has been very adroitly brought about. Summers, Faulkner, Preston and Berry, also Campbell and Brook will be fast friends to the measure. They are talented young men and will manage this affair most excellently well.

Tenth day. The slave question increases.

Eleventh day. Hopes are entertained by my young friends that a debate can be had upon the slave question.

Twelfth day. Mr. Goode this day made a motion to discharge the Committee on so much of the Governor's message as relates to free negroes and mulattoes and to which a memorial of sundry citizens of Hanover had been referred with a view to prevent debate upon the Slave question involved in that memorial. The abolition party opposed it and hence the slave party have produced the very debate they wished to avoid, and too, have entered upon it with open doors.

Thirteenth day. The debate in the House of Delegates still continues.

Fifteenth day. The debate in the House continued with great ability by Faulkner. This is a fine talented young gentleman.

Sixteenth day. The debate continues with increased ability. . . .

Nineteenth day. The debate still goes on.

Twentieth day. Nothing now is talked of or creates any interest but debate on the abolition of slavery. All is well.

Twenty-first day. The debate in the House is growing in interest and fear engendering bad and party feelings. It must be checked in erratic tendencies.

Twenty-third day. Many speculations are now made upon the result of this debate. We can carry the question, if necessary, by about two votes which will depend upon the views and objects to be developed by the slave part of the state. I think as yet nothing has transpired other than to prove that they must not be hurt, but held in check.

Twenty-fourth day. The debate begins to be carried on in an angry tone. It is not good that it should be so.

Twenty-fifth day. The debate is stopped but the members from South side of the James River talk of making a proposition to divide the State by the Blue Ridge Mountains sooner than part with their negroes which is the property of that part of the State.

Twenty-sixth day. The talk of dividing the State continues.

13

Letter from Virginia Governor John Floyd to South Carolina Governor James Hamilton Jr.

November 19, 1831

Floyd's letter to South Carolina governor James Hamilton contained the clearest and most complete statement of his belief that the Nat Turner rebellion was caused by Northerners—peddlers, traders, preachers, and abolitionists. Floyd singled out black preachers as a particularly dangerous group. Moreover, he expressed his interest in a plan for gradual emancipation and outlined a set of policies intended to prevent future rebellions. There is no record of Hamilton's response to Floyd's letter, but it is likely he was horrified by his fellow governor's support for gradual emancipation.

Richmond
November 19, 1831

Sir:

I received your letter yesterday and with great pleasure will give you my impressions freely—

I will notice this affair in my annual message, but here only give a very careless history of it, as it appeared to the public—

I am fully persuaded, the spirit of insubordination which has, and still manifests itself in Virginia, had its origin among, and eminated from,

---

The original of Floyd's letter to Hamilton can be found in the Manuscript Division of the Library of Congress.

the Yankee population, upon their *first* arrival amongst us, but mostly especially the Yankee pedlers and traders.

The course has been by no means a direct one—they began first, by making them religious—their conversations were of that character—telling the blacks, God was no respecter of persons—the black man was as good as the white—that all men were born free and equal—that they cannot serve two masters—that the white people rebelled against England to obtain freedom, so have the blacks a right to do.

In the mean time, I am sure without any purpose of this kind, the preachers, principally Northern—were very assiduous in operating upon our population, day and night, they were at work—and religion became, and is, the fashion of the times—finally our females and of the most respectable were persuaded that it was piety to teach negroes to read and write, to the end that they might read the *Scriptures*—many of them became tutoresses in Sunday schools and, pious distributors of tracts, from the New York Tract Society.

At this point, more active operations commenced—our magistrates and laws became more inactive—large assemblages of negroes were suffered to take place for religious purposes—Then commenced the efforts of the black preachers, often from the pulpits these pamphlets and papers were read—followed by the incendiary publications of Walker, Garrison and Knapp[1] of Boston, these too with songs and hymns of a similar character were circulated, read and commented upon—We resting in apathetic security until the Southampton affair.

From all that has come to my knowledge during and since this affair—I am fully convinced that every black preacher in the whole country east of the Blue Ridge was in the secret, that the plans as published by those Northern presses were adopted and acted upon by them—that their congregations, as they were called knew nothing of this intended rebellion, except a few leading and intelligent men, who may have been head men in the Church—*the mass* were prepared by making them aspire to an equal station by such conversations as I have related as the first step.

I am informed that they had settled the form of government to be that of white people, whom they intended to cut off to a man—with the difference that the preachers were to be their Governors, Generals and Judges. I feel fully justified to myself, in believing the Northern incendiaries, tracts, Sunday Schools, religion and reading and writing has accomplished this end.

---

[1]Probably a reference to Isaac Knapp (1804–1843), William Lloyd Garrison's partner as publisher of the abolitionist newspaper *The Liberator*.

I shall in my annual message recommend that laws be passed—To confine the Slaves to the estates of their masters—prohibit negroes from preaching—absolutely to drive from this State all free negroes—and to substitute the surplus revenue in our Treasury annually for slaves, to work for a time upon our Rail Roads etc etc and these sent out of the country, preparatory, or rather as the first step to emancipation—This last point will of course be tenderly and cautiously managed and will be urged or delayed as your State and Georgia may be disposed to co-operate.

In relation to the extent of this insurrection I think it greater than will ever appear—the facts will as now considered, appear to be these—It commenced with Nat and nine others on Sunday night—two o'clock, we date it, Monday morning before day and ceased by the dispersion of the negroes on Tuesday morning at ten o'clock—During this time the negroes had murdered sixty one persons, and traversed a distance of twenty miles, and increased to about seventy slave men—they spared but one family and that one was so wretched as to be in all respects upon a par with them—all died bravely indicating no reluctance to loose [*sic*] their lives in such a cause.

I am Sir,
with consideration and respect
Your obt Sevnt

John Floyd

His Excy
   James Hamilton, Jr.
      Governor of South Carolina

14

THOMAS R. DEW

Abolition of Negro Slavery

September and December 1832

Thomas Roderick Dew was only thirty years old when he wrote his analysis of the Virginia legislature's 1831–1832 debate on emancipation. But he was already a well-respected professor of political law at the College of William and Mary. Dew was a joint product of the social world of Tidewater Virginia and the intellectual world of the College of William and Mary. He grew up in a community of masters and enslaved people, attended the College of William and Mary through completion of a master's degree, and was appointed professor in 1826.

Dew's analysis of the Virginia debates became a classic in the larger body of literature known as the proslavery argument. It was first published in the American Quarterly Review *under the title "Abolition of Negro Slavery." This is the version reproduced here, because it was written in close proximity to the Nat Turner rebellion and it focuses on the issues discussed in the legislative debate on emancipation. Soon after, an expanded version of the essay containing a more elaborate general defense of slavery appeared as a separate publication under the title* Review of the Debate in the Virginia Legislature of 1831 and 1832. *The essay was later included in a classic compendium of proslavery writings published in 1852,* The Pro-Slavery Argument as Maintained by the Most Distinguished Writers of the Southern States.

Dew's essay offers a good summary of the reasons the Virginia legislature never adopted an emancipation plan. His central focus is on the impracticality of all emancipation schemes—whether emancipation with deportation of freed people or emancipation with freed people remaining in the state. Any abolition, Dew argued, would bring economic and social collapse to Virginia society. Included below are excerpts from Dew's essay.

Thomas R. Dew, "Abolition of Negro Slavery," *American Quarterly Review* 12 (September and December 1832).

In our southern slave-holding country, the question of emancipation had never been seriously discussed in any of our legislatures until the whole subject, under the most exciting circumstances, was, during the last winter, brought up for discussion in the Virginia legislature, and plans of partial or total abolition were earnestly pressed upon the attention of that body. It is well known, that during the last summer in the county of Southampton in Virginia, a few slaves, led on by Nat Turner, rose in the night, and murdered in the most inhuman and shocking manner between sixty and seventy of the unsuspecting whites of that county. The news of course was rapidly diffused, and with it consternation and dismay were spread throughout the state, destroying for a time all feeling of security and confidence, and even when subsequent development had proven, that the conspiracy had originated with a fanatic negro preacher, (whose confessions prove beyond a doubt mental aberration,) and that this conspiracy embraced but slaves, all of whom had paid the penalty of their crimes, still the excitement remained, still the repose of the commonwealth was disturbed, for the ghastly horrors of the Southampton tragedy could not immediately be banished from the mind. *Rumour*, with her thousand tongues, was busily engaged in spreading tales of disaffection, plots, insurrections, and even massacres, which frightened the timid, and harassed and mortified the whole of the slaveholding population. During this period of excitement, when reason was almost banished from the mind, and the imagination was suffered to conjure up the most appalling phantoms, and picture to itself a crisis in the vista of futurity, when the overwhelming numbers of the blacks would rise superior to all restraint, and involve the finest portion of our land in universal ruin and desolation, we are not to wonder that even in the lower part of Virginia many should have seriously inquired, if this supposed monstrous evil could not be removed from her bosom. Some looked to the removal of the free people of colour, by the efforts of the Colonization Society,[1] as an antidote to all our ills; some were disposed to strike at the root of the evil, to call on the general government for aid, and by the labours of *Hercules* to extirpate the curse of slavery from the land; and others again, who could not bear that Virginia should stand towards the general government (whose unconstitutional action she had ever been foremost to resist) in the attitude of a suppliant, looked forward to the legislative action of the state as capable of achieving the desired result. In this degree of excitement and apprehension, the

---

[1]The American Colonization Society was founded in 1816 with the intention of encouraging and assisting free blacks and newly freed people to return to Africa.

legislature met, and plans for abolition were proposed and earnestly advocated in debate. . . .

We are very ready to admit, that in point of ability and eloquence, the debate transcended our expectations. One of the leading political papers in the state remarked — "We have never heard any debate so eloquent, so sustained, and in which so great a number of speakers had appeared, and commanded the attention of so numerous and intelligent an audience. Day after day multitudes throng to the capital, and have been compensated by eloquence which would have illustrated Rome or Athens." But however fine might have been the rhetorical display, however ably some isolated points might have been discussed, still we affirm, with confidence, that no enlarged, wise, and practical plan of operations, was proposed by the abolitionists. We will go further, and assert that their arguments, in most cases, were of a wild and intemperate character, based upon false principles, and assumptions of the most vicious and alarming kind, subversive of the rights of property and the order and tranquility of society, and portending to the whole slave-holding country — if they ever shall be followed out in practice — inevitable and ruinous consequences. Far be it, however, from us, to accuse the abolitionists in the Virginia legislature of any settled malevolent design to overturn or convulse the fabric of society. We have no doubt that they were acting conscientiously for the best; but it often happens that frail imperfect man, in the too ardent and confident pursuit of imaginary good, runs upon his utter destruction.

We have not formed our opinion lightly upon this subject; we have given to the vital question of abolition the most mature and intense consideration which we are capable of bestowing, and we have come to the conclusion — a conclusion which seems to be sustained by facts and reasoning as irresistible as the demonstration of the mathematician — that every plan of emancipation and deportation which we can possibly conceive, is *totally* impracticable. We shall endeavor to prove, that the attempt to execute these plans can only have a tendency to increase all the evils of which we complain, as resulting from slavery. If this be true, then the great question of abolition will necessarily be reduced to the question of emancipation, with a permission to remain, which we think can easily be shown to be subversive of the interests, security, and happiness, of both the blacks and whites, and consequently hostile to every principle of expediency, morality, and religion. We have heretofore doubted the propriety even of too frequently agitating, especially in a public manner, the questions of abolition, in consequence of the injurious effects which might be produced on the slave population. But the Virginia legislature, in its zeal for discussion, boldly set aside all prudential considerations of this kind, and openly and publicly debated the subject before the whole world. The seal has now been broken, the example has been set from a high quarter; we shall, therefore, waive all considerations of a prudential character which have heretofore restrained us, and boldly grapple with the abolitionists on this great question. We fear not the result, so far as truth, justice, and expediency alone are concerned. But we must be permitted to say, that we do most deeply dread the effects of misguided philanthropy, and the intrusion, in this matter, of those who have no interest at stake, and who have not that intimate and minute knowledge of the whole subject so absolutely necessary to wise action. . . .

In our study, we began the examination of this subject with a general inquiry into the origin of slavery in ancient and modern times, and proceeded to a consideration of the slave trade, by which slavery has been introduced into the United States. We indicated the true sources of slavery, and the principles upon which it rests, in order that the value of those arguments founded on the maxims that "all men are born equal," that "slavery in the abstract is wrong," that "the slave has a natural right to regain his liberty," and so forth, might be fully appreciated. We endeavoured to show that those maxims may be and generally are inapplicable and mischievous, and that something else is requisite to convert slavery into freedom, than the mere enunciation of abstract truths divested of all adventitious circumstances and relations. But this first principal division of our subject proved so voluminous that we have been obliged to set it aside for the present, in order to obtain room for the more pressing and important topics of the great question which we undertook to treat. Upon these we enter, therefore, at once, and inquire seriously and fairly whether there be means by which our country may get rid of negro slavery.

Plans for the Abolition of Slavery

Under this head we will consider, first, those schemes which propose abolition and deportation, and secondly, those which contemplate emancipation without deportation. 1st. In the late Virginia legislature, where the subject of slavery underwent the most thorough discussion, all seemed to be perfectly agreed in the necessity of removal in case of emancipation. Several members from the lower counties, which are deeply interested in this question, seemed to be sanguine in their anticipations of the final success of some project of emancipation and deportation to Africa, the original home of the negro. "Let us translate them," said one of the most respected and able members of the Legislature, (Gen. Broadnax,) "to those realms from which, in evil times, under inauspicious influences, their fathers were unfortunately abducted.—Mr. Speaker, the idea of restoring these people to the region in which nature had planted them, and to whose climate she had fitted their constitutions—the idea of benefiting not only our condition and their condition by the removal, but making them the means of carrying back to a great continent, lost in the profoundest depths of savage barbarity, unconscious of the existence even of the God who created them, not only the arts and comforts and multiplied advantages of civilized life, but what is of more value than all, a knowledge of true religion—intelligence of a Redeemer—is one of the grandest and noblest, one of the most expansive and glorious ideas which ever entered into the imagination of man. The conception, whether to the philosopher, the statesman, the philanthropist, or the Christian, of rearing up a colony which is to be the nucleus around which future emigration will concenter, and open all Africa to civilization and commerce, and science and arts and religion—when Ethiopia shall stretch out her hands, indeed, is one which warms the heart with delight." . . . We fear that this splendid vision, the creation of a brilliant imagination, influenced by the pure feelings of a philanthropic and generous heart, is destined to vanish at the severe touch of analysis. Fortunately for reason and common sense, all these projects of deportation may be subjected to the most rigid and accurate calculations, which are amply sufficient to dispel all doubt, even in the minds of the most sanguine, as to their practicability.

We take it for granted that the right of the owner to his slave is to be respected, and consequently that he is not required to emancipate him, unless his full value is paid by the state. Let us then, keeping this in view, proceed to the very simple calculation of the expense of emancipation and deportation in Virginia. The slaves, by the last census (1830) amounted within a small fraction to 470,000; the average value of each one of these is $200; consequently the whole agregate value of the slave population of Virginia in 1830, was $94,000,000, and allowing for the increase since, we cannot err far in putting the present value at $100,000,000. The assessed value of all the houses and lands in the state amounts to $206,000,000, and these constitute the material items in the wealth of the state, the whole personal property besides bearing but a very small proportion to the value of slaves, lands, and houses. Now, do not these very simple statistics speak volumes upon this subject? It is gravely recommended to the state of Virginia to give up a species of property which constitutes nearly one-third of the wealth of the whole state, and almost one-half of that of Lower Virginia, and with the remaining two-thirds to encounter the additional enormous expense of transportation and colonization on the coast of Africa. But the loss of $100,000,000 of property is scarcely the half of what Virginia would lose, if the immutable laws of nature could suffer (as fortunately they cannot) this tremendous scheme of colonization to be carried into full effect. Is it not population which makes our lands and houses valuable? Why are lots in Paris and London worth more than the silver dollars which it might take to cover them? Why are lands of equal fertility in England and France worth more than those of our Northern States, and again worth more than Southern soils, and those in turn worth more than the soils of the distant West? It is the presence or absence of population which alone can explain the fact. It is in truth the slave labour in Virginia which gives value to her soil and her habitations. . . .

But the favourers of this scheme say they do not contend for the sudden emancipation and deportation of the whole black population; — they would send off only the increase, and thereby keep down the population to its present amount, while the whites increasing at their usual rate would finally become relatively so numerous as to render the presence of the blacks among us for ever afterwards entirely harmless. This scheme, which at first to the unreflecting seems plausible, and much less wild than the project of sending off the whole, is nevertheless impracticable and visionary, as we think a few remarks will prove. It is computed that the annual increase of the slaves and free coloured population of Virginia is about six thousand. Let us first, then, make a calculation of the expense of purchase and transportation. At $200 each, the six thousand will amount in value to $1,200,000. At $30 each, for transportation, which we shall soon see is too little, we have the whole expense of purchase and transportation $1,380,000, an expense to be annually incurred by Virginia to keep down her black population to its present amount. And let us ask, is there any one who can seriously argue that Virginia can incur such an annual expense as this for the next twenty-five or fifty years, until the whites have multiplied so greatly upon the blacks, as in the *opinion* of the *alarmists* for ever to quiet the fears of the community? . . .

But this does not develop to its full extent the monstrous absurdity of this scheme. There is a view of it yet to be taken, which seems not to have struck very forcibly any of the speakers in the Virginia legislature, but which appears to us of itself perfectly conclusive against this whole project. We have made some efforts to obtain something like an accurate account of the number of negroes every year carried out of

Virginia to the south and south-west. We have not been enabled to succeed completely; but from all the information we can obtain, we have no
hesitation in saying, that upwards of six thousand are yearly exported to
other states. Virginia is in fact a *negro* raising state for other states; she
produces enough for her own supply and six thousand for sale. Now, suppose the government of Virginia enters the slave market, resolved to
purchase six thousand for emancipation and deportation, is it not evi-
dent that it must overbid the southern seeker, and thus take the very
slaves who would have gone to the south? The very first operation then
of this scheme, provided slaves be treated as property, is to arrest the
current which has been hitherto flowing to the south, and to accumulate
the evil in the state. . . .

. . . Now looking at the texture of the Virginia population, the desid-
eratum[2] is to diminish the blacks and increase the whites. Let us see
how the scheme of emancipation and deportation will act. We have
already shown that the first operation of the plan, if slave property were
rigidly respected and never taken without full compensation, would be
to put a stop to the efflux from the state through other channels; but
this would not be the only effect. Government entering into the market
with individuals, would elevate the price of slaves beyond their natural
value, and consequently the raising of them would become an object of
primary importance throughout the whole state. We can readily imagine that the price of slaves might become so great that each master
would do all in his power to encourage marriage among them—would
allow the females almost entire exemption from labour, that they might
the better breed and nurse—and would so completely concentrate his
efforts upon this object, as to neglect other schemes and less productive sources of wealth. Under these circumstances the prolific African
might no doubt be stimulated to press hard upon one of the limits above
stated, doubling his numbers in fifteen years; and such is the tendency
which our abolition schemes, if ever seriously engaged in, will most
undoubtedly produce; they will be certain to stimulate the procreative
powers of that very race which they are aiming to diminish; they will
enlarge and invigorate the very monster which they are endeavouring
to stifle, and realize the beautiful but melancholy fable of Sisyphus, by an
eternal renovation of hope and disappointment. . . .

But our opponents perhaps may be disposed to answer, that this
increase of slavery from the stimulus to the black population afforded by
the colonization abroad, ought not to be objected to on our own prin-

[2]Something wanted or needed.

ciples, since each slave will be worth two hundred dollars or more. This answer would be correct enough if it were not that the increase of the blacks is effected at our expense both as to wealth and numbers; and to show this, we will now proceed to point out the operation of the scheme under consideration upon the white population. Malthus has clearly shown that population depends on the *means of subsistence*, and will, under ordinary circumstances, increase to a level with them. Now by means of subsistence we must not only comprehend the necessaries of life, such as food, clothing, shelter, &c., but likewise such conveniences, comforts, and even luxuries, as the habits of the society may render it essential for all to enjoy. Whatever then has a tendency to destroy the wealth and diminish the aggregate capital of society, has the effect, as long as the *standard of comfort** remains the same, to check the progress of the population.

It is sure to discourage matrimony, and cause children to be less carefully attended to, and to be less abundantly supplied. The heavy burthens which have hitherto been imposed on Virginia, through the operation of Federal exactions, together with the *high standard* of comfort prevalent throughout the whole state, (about which we shall by and by make a few observations) have already imposed checks upon the progress of the white population of the state. If not one single individual were to emigrate from the state of Virginia, it would be found, so inert has become the principle of increase in the state, that the population would not advance with the average rapidity of the American people. Now, under these circumstances, an imposition of an additional burthen of $1,380,000 for the purpose of purchase and deportation of slaves, would add so much to the taxes of the citizens—would subtract so much from the capital of the state, and increase so greatly the embarrassments of the whole population, that fewer persons would be enabled to support families, and consequently to get married. This great tax, added to those we are already suffering under, would weigh like an incubus upon the whole state—it would operate like the blighting hand of Providence that should render our soil barren and our labour unproductive. It would diminish the value of the *fee simple*[3] of Virginia, and not only check the natural increase of population within the commonwealth, but would make every man desirous of quitting the scenes of his home and his infancy, and fleeing from the heavy burthen which would for ever

---

*By standard of comfort we mean that amount of necessaries, conveniencies, and luxuries, which the habits of any people render essential to them.

[3]The inheritance of landed wealth absolutely and without restriction.

keep him and his children buried in the depths of poverty. His sale of negroes would partly enable him to emigrate; and we have little doubt, that whenever this wild scheme shall be seriously commenced, it will be found that more whites than negroes will be banished by its operation from the state. And there will be this lamentable difference between those who are left behind; a powerful stimulus will be given to the procreative energies of the blacks, while those of the whites will be paralyzed and destroyed. Every emigrant from among the whites will create a vacuum not to be supplied — every removal of a black will stimulate to the generation of another. . . .

The *poverty* stricken master would rejoice in the prolificness of his female slave, but pray Heaven in its kindness to strike with barrenness his own spouse, lest in the plenitude of his misfortunes, brought on by the wild and Quixotic philanthropy of his government, he might see around him a numerous offspring unprovided for and destined to galling indigence.

It is almost useless to inquire whether this deportation of slaves to Africa would, as some seem most strangely to anticipate, invite the whites of other states into the commonwealth. Who would be disposed to enter a state with worn out soil and a black population mortgaged to the payment of millions per annum, for the purpose of emancipation and deportation, when in the West the most luxuriant soils, unencumbered with heavy exactions could be purchased for the paltry sum of $1.25 per acre? . . .

There is $100,000,000 of slave property in the state of Virginia, and it matters but little how you destroy it, whether by the slow process of the cautious *practitioner*, or with the frightful dispatch of the self confident *quack*; when it is gone, no matter how, the deed will be done, and Virginia will be a desert.

15

DAVID WALKER

Appeal to the Coloured Citizens of the World
1830

The first edition of David Walker's Appeal *was published in Boston late in 1829. The third edition, excerpted here, dates from the spring of 1830. It is a cry of rage against slavery from an African American, and nothing else quite like it was written during the antebellum period.*

Walker himself was born a free man in Wilmington, North Carolina. At some point during the early 1820s, he moved to Charleston, South Carolina, where he probably joined the African Methodist Episcopal church that stood at the center of the Denmark Vesey conspiracy of 1822. After that church was destroyed, he traveled widely, ending up in Boston by 1825, where he became active in challenging racism and in organizing African Americans to attack slavery aggressively. He intended his Appeal *to stir African Americans, especially those who were enslaved, into action against slavery. He condemned the degrading impact of racism in the strongest possible terms, noted the impending threat of judgment on the white population from an angry and righteous God, and reminded blacks of their obligation to resist slavery even before God acted.*

Most significantly, Walker intended his Appeal *to be "read" by enslaved people in the South. He used his position as a buyer and seller of used clothing near the docks of Boston to find people who would carry his publication south, and he issued instructions for those who were literate to read his pamphlet aloud to those who could not read. Due to the diligent research of historian Peter Hinks, we know that the* Appeal *circulated during the period just before the Nat Turner rebellion in Savannah and Milledgeville, Georgia; Richmond, Virginia; Charleston, South Carolina; New Orleans, Louisiana; and in and around Wilmington, North Carolina.*

We have no evidence that Nat Turner himself actually read the Appeal, *but it is important for students of the Nat Turner rebellion to be*

Preamble and Article I from David Walker, *Walker's Appeal, in Four Articles; Together with a Preamble, to the Coloured Citizens of the World, but in Particular, and Very Expressly, to Those of the United States of America, Written in Boston, State of Massachusetts, September 28, 1829*, 3rd ed. (Boston: David Walker, 1830).

aware of its content and influence. First, many Southern whites believed that Turner was influenced by Walker and by other abolitionists (see Document 13), and they acted on that belief. Second, the document circulated close enough to Southampton County so that it is possible that the contents could have been orally transmitted. Third, there is a striking similarity between Turner's and Walker's worldviews—with an impending millennial moment for a just God to punish racists and those who enslaved people, and a call for African Americans to begin to take action against slavery as a precursor to Judgment Day. This suggests the possibility that Turner and Walker could have been part of the same intellectual tradition even if neither was aware of it. The God of Nat Turner could have been the God of David Walker. The excerpt below includes Walker's introductory editorial notes, the Preamble, and Article I. The full original document consists of four Articles.

Note on the text: In the document that follows, minor typographical errors in the original have been corrected silently.

Walker's Editorial Notes for the Third Edition

It will be recollected, that I, in the first edition of my "Appeal,"* promised to demonstrate in the course of which, viz. in the course of my Appeal, to the satisfaction of the most incredulous mind, that we Coloured People of these United States, are, the most wretched, degraded and abject set of beings that ever lived since the world began, down to the present day, and, that, the white Christians of America, who hold us in slavery, (or, more properly speaking, pretenders to Christianity,) treat us more cruel and barbarous than any Heathen nation did any people whom it had subjected, or reduced to the same condition, that the Americans (who are, notwithstanding, looking for the Millennial day) have us. All I ask is, for a candid and careful perusal of this the third and last edition of my Appeal, where the world may see that we, the Blacks or Coloured People, are treated more cruel by the white Christians of America, than devils themselves ever treated a set of men, women and children on this earth.

It is expected that all coloured men, women and children,** of every nation, language and tongue under heaven, will try to procure a copy of this Appeal and read it, or get some one to read it to them, for it is

---

*See my Preamble in first edition, first page. See also 2d edition, Article 1, page 9.

**Who are not too deceitful, abject, and servile to resist the cruelties and murders inflicted upon us by the white slave holders, our enemies by nature.

designed more particularly for them. Let them remember, that though our cruel oppressors and murderers, may (if possible) treat us more cruel, as Pharaoh did the children of Israel, yet the God of the Ethiopians, has been pleased to hear our moans in consequence of oppression; and the day of our redemption from abject wretchedness draweth near, when we shall be enabled, in the most extended sense of the word, to stretch forth our hands to the LORD our GOD, but there must be a willingness on our part, for GOD to do these things for us, for we may be assured that he will not take us by the hairs of our head against our will and desire, and drag us from our very mean, low and abject condition.

Preamble

My dearly beloved Brethren and Fellow Citizens.

HAVING travelled over a considerable portion of these United States, and having, in the course of my travels, taken the most accurate observations of things as they exist—the result of my observations has warranted the full and unshaken conviction, that we, (coloured people of these United States,) are the most degraded, wretched, and abject set of beings that ever lived since the world began; and I pray God that none like us ever may live again until time shall be no more. They tell us of the Israelites in Egypt, the Helots in Sparta, and of the Roman Slaves, which last were made up from almost every nation under heaven, whose sufferings under those ancient and heathen nations, were, in comparison with ours, under this enlightened and Christian nation, no more than a cypher—or, in other words, those heathen nations of antiquity, had but little more among them than the name and form of slavery; while wretchedness and endless miseries were reserved, apparently in a phial, to be poured out upon our fathers, ourselves and our children, by *Christian* Americans!

These positions I shall endeavour, by the help of the Lord, to demonstrate in the course of this *Appeal*, to the satisfaction of the most incredulous mind—and may God Almighty, who is the Father of our Lord Jesus Christ, open your hearts to understand and believe the truth.

The *causes*, my brethren, which produce our wretchedness and miseries, are so very numerous and aggravating, that I believe the pen only of a Josephus or a Plutarch, can well enumerate and explain them. Upon subjects, then, of such incomprehensible magnitude, so impenetrable, and so notorious, I shall be obliged to omit a large class of, and content myself with giving you an exposition of a few of those, which do indeed rage to such an alarming pitch, that they cannot but be a perpetual source of terror and dismay to every reflecting mind.

I am fully aware, in making this appeal to my much afflicted and suffering brethren, that I shall not only be assailed by those whose greatest earthly desires are, to keep us in abject ignorance and wretchedness, and who are of the firm conviction that Heaven has designed us and our children to be slaves and *beasts of burden* to them and their children. I say, I do not only expect to be held up to the public as an ignorant, impudent and restless disturber of the public peace, by such avaricious creatures, as well as a mover of insubordination—and perhaps put in prison or to death, for giving a superficial exposition of our miseries, and exposing tyrants. But I am persuaded, that many of my brethren, particularly those who are ignorantly in league with slaveholders or tyrants, who acquire their daily bread by the blood and sweat of their more ignorant brethren—and not a few of those too, who are too ignorant to see an inch beyond their noses, will rise up and call me cursed—Yea, the jealous ones among us will perhaps use more abject subtlety, by affirming that this work is not worth perusing, that we are well situated, and there is no use in trying to better our condition, for we cannot. I will ask one question here.—Can our condition be any worse?—Can it be more mean and abject? If there are any changes, will they not be for the better, though they may appear for the worst at first? Can they get us any lower? Where can they get us? They are afraid to treat us worse, for they know well, the day they do it they are gone. But against all accusations which may or can be preferred against me, I appeal to Heaven for my motive in writing—who knows that my object is, if possible, to awaken in the breasts of my afflicted, degraded and slumbering brethren, a spirit of inquiry and investigation respecting our miseries and wretchedness in this *Republican Land of Liberty!!!!!!*

The sources from which our miseries are derived, and on which I shall comment, I shall not combine in one, but shall put them under distinct heads and expose them in their turn; in doing which, keeping truth on my side, and not departing from the strictest rules of morality, I shall endeavour to penetrate, search out, and lay them open for your inspection. If you cannot or will not profit by them, I shall have done *my* duty to you, my country and my God.

And as the inhuman system of *slavery*, is the *source* from which most of our miseries proceed, I shall begin with that *curse to nations*, which has spread terror and devastation through so many nations of antiquity, and which is raging to such a pitch at the present day in Spain and in Portugal. It had one tug in England, in France, and in the United States of America; yet the inhabitants thereof, do not learn wisdom, and erase it entirely from their dwellings and from all with whom they have to do.

The fact is, the labour of slaves comes so cheap to the avaricious usurpers, and is (as they think) of such great utility to the country where it exists, that those who are actuated by sordid avarice only, overlook the evils, which will as sure as the Lord lives, follow after the good. In fact, they are so happy to keep in ignorance and degradation, and to receive the homage and the labour of the slaves, they forget that God rules in the armies of heaven and among the inhabitants of the earth, having his ears continually open to the cries, tears and groans of his oppressed people; and being a just and holy Being will at one day appear fully in behalf of the oppressed, and arrest the progress of the avaricious oppressors; for although the destruction of the oppressors God may not effect by the oppressed, yet the Lord our God will bring other destructions upon them—for not unfrequently will he cause them to rise up one against another, to be split and divided, and to oppress each other, and sometimes to open hostilities with sword in hand. Some may ask, what is the matter with this united and happy people?—Some say it is the cause of political usurpers, tyrants, oppressors, &c. But has not the Lord an oppressed and suffering people among them? Does the Lord condescend to hear their cries and see their tears in consequence of oppression? Will he let the oppressors rest comfortably and happy always? Will he not cause the very children of the oppressors to rise up against them, and oftimes put them to death? "God works in many ways his wonders to perform."

I will not here speak of the destructions which the Lord brought upon Egypt, in consequence of the oppression and consequent groans of the oppressed—of the hundreds and thousands of Egyptians whom God hurled into the Red Sea for afflicting his people in their land—of the Lord's suffering people in Sparta or Lacedemon, the land of the truly famous Lycurgus—nor have I time to comment upon the cause which produced the fierceness with which Sylla usurped the title, and absolutely acted as dictator of the Roman people—the conspiracy of Cataline—the conspiracy against, and murder of Cæsar in the Senate house—the spirit with which Marc Antony made himself master of the commonwealth—his associating Octavius and Lipidus with himself in power—their dividing the provinces of Rome among themselves—their attack and defeat, on the plains of Phillippi, of the last defenders of their liberty, (Brutus and Cassius)—the tyranny of Tiberius, and from him to the final overthrow of Constantinople by the Turkish Sultan, Mahomed II. A.D. 1453. I say, I shall not take up time to speak of the *causes* which produced so much wretchedness and massacre among those heathen nations, for I am aware that you know too well, that God is just, as well as merciful!—I shall call your attention a few moments to that *Christian* nation, the Spaniards—while I shall leave almost unnoticed, that avaricious and cruel people, the Portuguese, among whom all true hearted Christians and lovers of Jesus Christ, must evidently see the judgments of God displayed. To show the judgments of God upon the Spaniards, I shall occupy but a little time, leaving plenty of room for the candid and unprejudiced to reflect.

All persons who are acquainted with history, and particularly the Bible, who are not blinded by the God of this world, and are not actuated solely by avarice—who are able to lay aside prejudice long enough to view candidly and impartially, things as they were, are, and probably will be—who are willing to admit that God made man to serve Him *alone*, and that man should have no other Lord or Lords but Himself—that God Almighty is the *sole proprietor* or *master* of the WHOLE human family, and will not on any consideration admit of a colleague, being unwilling to divide his glory with another—and who can dispense with prejudice long enough to admit that we are *men*, notwithstanding our *improminent noses* and *woolly heads*, and believe that we feel for our fathers, mothers, wives and children, as well as the whites do for theirs.—I say, all who are permitted to see and believe these things, can easily recognize the judgments of God among the Spaniards. Though others may lay the cause of the fierceness with which they cut each other's throats, to some other circumstance, yet they who believe that God is a God of justice, will believe that SLAVERY *is the principal cause.*

While the Spaniards are running about upon the field of battle cutting each other's throats, has not the Lord an afflicted and suffering people in the midst of them, whose cries and groans in consequence of oppression are continually pouring into the ears of the God of justice? Would they not cease to cut each other's throats, if they could? But how can they? The very support which they draw from government to aid them in perpetrating such enormities, does it not arise in a great degree from the wretched victims of oppression among them? And yet they are calling for *Peace!—Peace!!* Will any peace be given unto them? Their destruction may indeed be procrastinated awhile, but can it continue long, while they are oppressing the Lord's people? Has He not the hearts of all men in His hand? Will he suffer one part of his creatures to go on oppressing another like brutes always, with impunity? And yet, those avaricious wretches are calling for *Peace!!!!* I declare, it does appear to me, as though some nations think God is asleep, or that he made the Africans for nothing else but to dig their mines and work their farms, or they cannot believe history, sacred or profane. I ask every man who has a heart, and is blessed with the privilege of believing—Is not God a God of justice to *all* his creatures? Do you say he is? Then if he gives peace and tranquillity to tyrants, and permits them to keep our fathers, our mothers, ourselves and our children in eternal ignorance and wretchedness, to support them and their families, would he be to us a God of *justice*? I ask, O ye *Christians!!!* who hold us and our children in the most abject ignorance and degradation, that ever a people were afflicted with since the world began—I say, if God gives you peace and tranquillity, and suffers you thus to go on afflicting us, and our children, who have never given you the least provocation—would he be to us *a God of justice*? If you will allow that we are MEN, who feel for each other, does not the blood of our fathers and of us their children, cry aloud to the Lord of Sabaoth against you, for the cruelties and murders with which you have, and do continue to afflict us. But it is time for me to close my remarks on the suburbs, just to enter more fully into the interior of this system of cruelty and oppression.

Article I

OUR WRETCHEDNESS IN CONSEQUENCE OF SLAVERY

My beloved brethren:—The Indians of North and of South America— the Greeks—the Irish, subjected under the king of Great Britain—the Jews, that ancient people of the Lord—the inhabitants of the islands of the sea—in fine, all the inhabitants of the earth, (except however, the sons of Africa) are called *men*, and of course are, and ought to be free. But we, (coloured people) and our children are *brutes!!* and of course are, and *ought to be* SLAVES to the American people and their children forever!! to dig their mines and work their farms; and thus go on enriching them, from one generation to another with our *blood* and our *tears!!!!*

I promised in a preceding page to demonstrate to the satisfaction of the most incredulous, that we, (coloured people of these United States of America) are the *most wretched, degraded* and *abject* set of beings that *ever lived* since the world began, and that the white Americans having reduced us to the wretched state of *slavery*, treat us in that condition *more cruel* (they being an enlightened and Christian people), than any heathen nation did any people whom it had reduced to our condition. These affirmations are so well confirmed in the minds of all unprejudiced men, who have taken the trouble to read histories, that they need no elucidation from me. But to put them beyond all doubt, I refer you in the first place to the children of Jacob, or of Israel in Egypt, under Pharaoh and his people. Some of my brethren do not know who Pharaoh and the Egyptians were—I know it to be a fact, that some of them take the Egyptians to have been a gang of *devils*, not knowing any better, and that they (Egyptians) having got possession of the Lord's people, treated them *nearly* as cruel as *Christian Americans* do us, at the present day. For the information of such, I would only mention that the Egyptians were Africans or coloured people, such as we are—some of them yellow and others dark—a mixture of Ethiopians and the natives of Egypt—about the same as you see the coloured people of the United States at the present day.—I say, I call your attention then, to the children of Jacob, while I point out particularly to you his son Joseph, among the rest, in Egypt.

"And Pharaoh, said unto Joseph, thou shalt be over my house, and according unto thy word shall all my people be ruled: only in the throne will I be greater than thou."*

"And Pharaoh said unto Joseph, see, I have set thee over all the land of Egypt."**

"And Pharaoh said unto Joseph, I am Pharaoh, and without thee shall no man lift up his hand or foot in all the land of Egypt."***

Now I appeal to heaven and to earth, and particularly to the American people themselves, who cease not to declare that our condition is not *hard*, and that we are comparatively satisfied to rest in wretchedness and misery, under them and their children. Not, indeed, to show me a coloured President, a Governor, a Legislator, a Senator, a Mayor, or an Attorney at the Bar.—But to show me a man of colour, who holds the low office of a Constable, or one who sits in a Juror Box, even on a case of one of his wretched brethren, throughout this great Republic!!—But let us pass Joseph the son of Israel a little farther in review, as he existed with that heathen nation.

"And Pharaoh called Joseph's name Zaphnath-paaneah; and he gave him to wife Asenath the daughter of Potipherah priest of On. And Joseph went out over all the land of Egypt."**** Compare the above, with the American institutions. Do they not institute laws to prohibit us from marrying among the whites? I would wish, candidly, however, before the Lord, to be understood, that I would not give a *pinch of snuff* to be married to any white person I ever saw in all the days of my life. And I do say it, that the black man, or man of colour, who will leave his own

*See Genesis, chap. xli.
**xli. 44.
***xli. 45.
****xli. 45.

colour (provided he can get one, who is good for any thing) and marry a *white* woman, to be a double slave to her, just because she is white, ought to be treated by her as he surely will be, viz: as a NIGER!!!! It is not, indeed, what I care about inter-marriages with the whites, which induced me to pass this subject in review; for the Lord knows, that there is a day coming when they will be glad enough to get into the company of the blacks, notwithstanding, we are, in this generation, levelled by them, almost on a level with the brute creation: and some of us they treat even worse than they do the brutes that perish. I only made this extract to show how much lower we are held, and how much more cruel we are treated by the Americans, than were the children of Jacob, by the Egyptians.—We will notice the sufferings of Israel some further, under *heathen Pharaoh*, compared with ours under the *enlightened Christians of America*.

"And Pharaoh spake unto Joseph, saying, thy father and thy brethren are come unto thee:"

"The land of Egypt is before thee: in the best of the land make thy father and brethren to dwell; in the land of Goshen let them dwell: and if thou knowest any men of activity among them, then make them rulers over my cattle."*

I ask those people who treat us so *well*, Oh! I ask them, where is the most barren spot of land which they have given unto us? Israel had the most fertile land in all Egypt. Need I mention the very notorious fact, that I have known a poor man of colour, who laboured night and day, to acquire a little money, and having acquired it, he vested it in a small piece of land, and got him a house erected thereon, and having paid for the whole, he moved his family into it, where he was suffered to remain but nine months, when he was cheated out of his property by a white man, and driven out of door! And is not this the case generally? Can a man of colour buy a piece of land and keep it peaceably? Will not some white man try to get it from him, even if it is in a *mud hole*? I need not comment any farther on a subject, which all, both black and white, will readily admit. But I must, really, observe that in this very city, when a man of colour dies, if he owned any real estate it most generally falls into the hands of some white person. The wife and children of the deceased may weep and lament if they please, but the estate will be kept snug enough by its white possessor.

But to prove farther that the condition of the Israelites was better under the Egyptians than ours is under the whites. I call upon the professing Christians, I call upon the philanthropist, I call upon the very

*Genesis, chap. xlvii. 5, 6.

tyrant himself, to show me a page of history, either sacred or profane, on which a verse can be found, which maintains, that the Egyptians heaped the *insupportable insult* upon the children of Israel, by telling them that they were not of the *human family*. Can the whites deny this charge? Have they not, after having reduced us to the deplorable condition of slaves under their feet, held us up as descending originally from the tribes of *Monkeys* or *Orang- Outangs*? O! my God! I appeal to every man of feeling—is not this insupportable? Is it not heaping the most gross insult upon our miseries, because they have got us under their feet and we cannot help ourselves? Oh! pity us we pray thee, Lord Jesus, Master.—Has Mr. Jefferson[1] declared to the world, that we are inferior to the whites, both in the endowments of our bodies and of minds? It is indeed surprising, that a man of such great learning, combined with such excellent natural parts, should speak so of a set of men in chains. I do not know what to compare it to, unless, like putting one wild deer in an iron cage, where it will be secured, and hold another by the side of the same, then let it go, and expect the one in the cage to run as fast as the one at liberty. So far, my brethren, were the Egyptians from heaping these insults upon their slaves, that Pharaoh's daughter took Moses, a son of Israel for her own, as will appear by the following.

"And Pharaoh's daughter said unto her, [Moses' mother] take this child away, and nurse it for me, and I will pay thee thy wages. And the woman took the child [Moses] and nursed it."

"And the child grew, and she brought him unto Pharaoh's daughter and he became her son. And she called his name Moses: and she said because I drew him out of the water."*

In all probability, Moses would have become Prince Regent to the throne, and no doubt, in process of time but he would have been seated on the throne of Egypt. But he had rather suffer shame, with the people of God, than to enjoy pleasures with that wicked people for a season. O! that the coloured people were long since of Moses' excellent disposition, instead of courting favour with, and telling news and lies to our *natural enemies*, against each other—aiding them to keep their hellish chains of slavery upon us. Would we not long before this time, have been respectable men, instead of such wretched victims of oppression as we are? Would they be able to drag our mothers, our fathers, our wives, our children and ourselves, around the world in chains and hand-

[1] Walker refers here to former President Thomas Jefferson. He was deeply offended by Jefferson's racist arguments for black inferiority contained in his *Notes on the State of Virginia*.
*See Exodus, chap. ii. 9, 10.

cuffs as they do, to dig up gold and silver for them and theirs? This question, my brethren, I leave for you to digest; and may God Almighty force it home to your hearts. Remember that unless you are united, keeping your tongues within your teeth, you will be afraid to trust your secrets to each other, and thus perpetuate our miseries under the *Christians!!!!!* ADDITION.— Remember, also to lay humble at the feet of our Lord and Master Jesus Christ, with prayers and fastings. Let our enemies go on with their butcheries, and at once fill up their cup. Never make an attempt to gain our freedom of *natural right*, from under our cruel oppressors and murderers, until you see your way clear*—when that hour arrives and you move, be not afraid or dismayed; for be you assured that Jesus Christ the King of heaven and of earth who is the God of justice and of armies, will surely go before you. And those enemies who have for hundreds of years stolen our *rights*, and kept us ignorant of Him and His divine worship, he will remove. Millions of whom, are this day, so ignorant and avaricious, that they cannot conceive how God can have an attribute of justice, and show mercy to us because it pleased Him to make us black—which colour, Mr. Jefferson calls unfortunate!!!!!! As though we are not as thankful to our God, for having made us as it pleased himself, as they, (the whites,) are for having made them white. They think because they hold us in their infernal chains of slavery, that we wish to be white, or of their color—but they are dreadfully deceived—we wish to be just as it pleased our Creator to have made us, and no avaricious and unmerciful wretches, have any business to make slaves of, or hold us in slavery. How would they like for us to make slaves of, and hold them in cruel slavery, and murder them as they do us?—But is Mr. Jefferson's assertions true? viz. "that it is unfortunate for us that our Creator has been pleased to make us *black*." We will not take his say so, for the fact. The world will have an opportunity to see whether it is unfortunate for us, that our Creator *has made us* darker than the *whites*.

Fear not the number and education of our *enemies*, against whom we shall have to contend for our lawful right; guaranteed to us by our

---

*It is not to be understood here, that I mean for us to wait until God shall take us by the hair of our heads and drag us out of abject wretchedness and slavery, nor do I mean to convey the idea for us to wait until our enemies shall make preparations, and call us to seize those preparations, take it away from them, and put every thing before us to death, in order to gain our freedom which God has given us. For you must remember that we are men as well as they. God has been pleased to give us two eyes, two hands, two feet, and some sense in our heads as well as they. They have no more right to hold us in slavery than we have to hold them, we have just as much right, in the sight of God, to hold them and their children in slavery and wretchedness, as they have to hold us, and no more.

Maker; for why should we be afraid, when God is, and will continue, (if we continue humble) to be on our side?

The man who would not fight under our Lord and Master Jesus Christ, in the glorious and heavenly cause of freedom and of God—to be delivered from the most wretched, abject and servile slavery, that ever a people was afflicted with since the foundation of the world, to the present day—ought to be kept with all of his children or family, in slavery, or in chains, to be butchered by his *cruel enemies*.

I saw a paragraph, a few years since, in a South Carolina paper, which, speaking of the barbarity of the Turks, it said: "The Turks are the most barbarous people in the world—they treat the Greeks more like *brutes* than human beings." And in the same paper was an advertisement, which said: "Eight well built Virginia and Maryland *Negro fellows* and four *wenches* will positively be *sold* this day, *to the highest bidder!*" And what astonished me still more was, to see in this same *humane* paper!! the cuts of three men, with clubs and budgets on their backs, and an advertisement offering a considerable sum of money for their apprehension and delivery. I declare, it is really so amusing to hear the Southerners and Westerners of this country talk about *barbarity*, that it is positively, enough to make a man *smile*.

The sufferings of the Helots among the Spartans, were somewhat severe, it is true, but to say that theirs, were as severe as ours among the Americans, I do most strenuously deny—for instance, can any man show me an article on a page of ancient history which specifies, that, the Spartans chained, and hand-cuffed the Helots, and dragged them from their wives and children, children from their parents, mothers from their suckling babes, wives from their husbands, driving them from one end of the country to the other? Notice the Spartans were heathens, who lived long before our Divine Master made his appearance in the flesh. Can Christian Americans deny these barbarous cruelties? Have you not, Americans, having subjected us under you, added to these miseries, by insulting us in telling us to our face, because *we* are helpless, that *we* are not of the human family? I ask you, O! Americans, I ask you, in the name of the Lord, can you deny these charges? Some perhaps may deny, by saying, that they never thought or said that we were not men. But do not actions speak louder than words?—have they not made provisions for the Greeks, and Irish? Nations who have never done the least thing for them, while we, who have enriched their country with our blood and tears—have dug up gold and silver for them and their children, from generation to generation, and are in more miseries than any other people under heaven, are not seen, but by comparatively, a handful of the American people? There are indeed, more ways to kill a dog, besides choking it to death with butter. Further—The Spartans or Lacedaemonians, had some frivolous pretext, for enslaving the Helots, for they (Helots) while being free inhabitants of Sparta, stirred up an intestine commotion, and were, by the Spartans subdued, and made prisoners of war. Consequently they and their children were condemned to perpetual slavery.*

I have been for years troubling the pages of historians, to find out what our fathers have done to the *white Christians of America*, to merit such condign punishment as they have inflicted on them, and do continue to inflict on us their children. But I must aver, that my researches have hitherto been to no effect. I have therefore, come to the immoveable conclusion, that they (Americans) have, and do continue to punish us for nothing else, but for enriching them and their country. For I cannot conceive of any thing else. Nor will I ever believe otherwise, until the Lord shall convince me.

The world knows, that slavery as it existed among the Romans, (which was the primary cause of their destruction) was, comparatively speaking, no more than a *cypher*, when compared with ours under the Americans. Indeed I should not have noticed the Roman slaves, had not the very learned and penetrating Mr. Jefferson said, "when a master was murdered, all his slaves in the same house, or within hearing, were condemned to death."**—Here let me ask Mr. Jefferson, (but he is gone to answer at the bar of God, for the deeds done in his body while living,) I therefore ask the whole American people, had I not rather die, or be put to death, than to be a slave to any tyrant, who takes not only my own, but my wife and children's lives by the inches? Yea, would I meet death with avidity far! far!! in preference to such *servile submission* to the murderous hands of tyrants. Mr. Jefferson's very severe remarks on us have been so extensively argued upon by men whose attainments in literature, I shall never be able to reach, that I would not have meddled with it, were it not to solicit each of my brethren, who has the spirit of a man, to buy a copy of Mr. Jefferson's "Notes on Virginia," and put it in the hand of his son. For let no one of us suppose that the refutations which have been written by our white friends are enough—they are *whites*—we are *blacks*. We, and the world wish to see the charges of Mr. Jefferson refuted by the blacks *themselves*, according to their chance;

---

*See Dr. Goldsmith's History of Greece—page 9. See also, Plutarch's Lives. The Helots subdued by Agis, king of *Sparta*.

**See his Notes on Virginia, page 210.

for we must remember that what the whites have written respecting this subject, is other men's labours, and did not emanate from the blacks. I know well, that there are some talents and learning among the coloured people of this country, which we have not a chance to develope, in consequence of oppression; but our oppression ought not to hinder us from acquiring all we can. For we will have a chance to develope them by and by. God will not suffer us, always to be oppressed. Our sufferings will come to an *end*, in spite of all the Americans this side of *eternity*. Then we will want all the learning and talents among ourselves, and perhaps more, to govern ourselves. — "Every dog must have its day"[;] the American's is coming to an end.

But let us review Mr. Jefferson's remarks respecting us some further. Comparing our miserable fathers, with the learned philosophers of Greece, he says: "Yet notwithstanding these and other discouraging circumstances among the Romans, their slaves were often their rarest artists. They excelled too, in science, insomuch as to be usually employed as tutors to their master's children; Epictetus, Terence and Phædrus, were slaves, — but they were of the race of whites. It is not their *condition* then, but *nature*, which has produced the distinction."* See this, my brethren!! Do you believe that this assertion is swallowed by millions of the whites? Do you know that Mr. Jefferson was one of as great characters as ever lived among the whites? See his writings for the world, and public labours for the United States of America. Do you believe that the assertions of such a man, will pass away into oblivion unobserved by this people and the world? If you do you are much mistaken — See how the American people treat us — have we souls in our bodies? Are we men who have any spirits at all? I know that there are many *swell-bellied* fellows among us, whose greatest object is to fill their stomachs. Such I do not mean — I am after those who know and feel, that we are MEN, as well as other people; to them, I say, that unless we try to refute Mr. Jefferson's arguments respecting us, we will only establish them.

But the slaves among the Romans. Every body who has read history, knows, that as soon as a slave among the Romans obtained his freedom, he could rise to the greatest eminence in the State, and there was no law instituted to hinder a slave from buying his freedom. Have not the Americans instituted laws to hinder us from obtaining our freedom? Do any deny this charge? Read the laws of Virginia, North Carolina, &c. Further: have not the Americans instituted laws to prohibit a man of colour

*See his Notes on Virginia, page 211.

from obtaining and holding any office whatever, under the government of the United States of America? Now, Mr. Jefferson tells us, that our condition is not so hard, as the slaves were under the Romans!!!!!!

It is time for me to bring this article to a close. But before I close it, I must observe to my brethren that at the close of the first Revolution in this country, with Great Britain, there were but thirteen States in the Union, now there are twenty-four, most of which are slave-holding States, and the whites are dragging us around in chains and in handcuffs, to their new States and Territories to work their mines and farms, to enrich them and their children—and millions of them believing firmly that we being a little darker than they, were made by our Creator to be an inheritance to them and their children for ever—the same as a parcel of *brutes*.

Are we MEN!!—I ask you, O my brethren! are we MEN? Did our Creator make us to be slaves to dust and ashes like ourselves? Are they not dying worms as well as we? Have they not to make their appearance before the tribunal of Heaven, to answer for the deeds done in the body, as well as we? Have we any other Master but Jesus Christ alone? Is he not their Master as well as ours?—What right then, have we to obey and call any other Master, but Himself? How we could be so *submissive* to a gang of men, whom we cannot tell whether they are *as good* as ourselves or not, I never could conceive. However, this is shut up with the Lord, and we cannot precisely tell—but I declare, we judge men by their works.

The whites have always been an unjust, jealous, unmerciful, avaricious and blood-thirsty set of beings, always seeking after power and authority.—We view them all over the confederacy of Greece, where they were first known to be any thing, (in consequence of education) we see them there, cutting each other's throats—trying to subject each other to wretchedness and misery—to effect which, they used all kinds of deceitful, unfair, and unmerciful means. We view them next in Rome, where the spirit of tyranny and deceit raged still higher. We view them in Gaul, Spain, and in Britain.—In fine, we view them all over Europe, together with what were scattered about in Asia and Africa, as heathens, and we see them acting more like devils than accountable men. But some may ask, did not the blacks of Africa, and the mulattoes of Asia, go on in the same way as did the whites of Europe. I answer, no—they never were half so avaricious, deceitful and unmerciful as the whites, according to their knowledge.

But we will leave the whites or Europeans as heathens, and take a view of them as Christians, in which capacity we see them as cruel, if not more so than ever. In fact, take them as a body, they are ten times more cruel, avaricious and unmerciful than ever they were; for while they were heathens, they were bad enough it is true, but it is positively a fact that they were not quite so audacious as to go and take vessel loads of men, women and children, and in cold blood, and through devilishness, throw them into the sea, and murder them in all kind of ways. While they were heathens, they were too ignorant for such barbarity. But being Christians, enlightened and sensible, they are completely prepared for such hellish cruelties. Now suppose God were to give them more sense, what would they do? If it were possible, would they not *dethrone* Jehovah and seat themselves upon his throne? I therefore, in the name and fear of the Lord God of Heaven and of earth, divested of prejudice either on the side of my colour or that of the whites, advance my suspicion of them, whether they are *as good by nature* as we are or not. Their actions, since they were known as a people, have been the reverse, I do indeed suspect them, but this, as I before observed, is shut up with the Lord, we cannot exactly tell, it will be proved in succeeding generations.—The whites have had the essence of the gospel as it was preached by my master and his apostles—the Ethiopians have not, who are to have it in its meridian splendor—the Lord will give it to them to their satisfaction. I hope and pray my God, that they will make good use of it, that it may be well with them.*

---

*It is my solemn belief, that if ever the world becomes Christianized, (which must certainly take place before long) it will be through the means, under God of the *Blacks*, who are now held in wretchedness, and degradation, by the white *Christians* of the world, who before they learn to do justice to us before our Maker—and be reconciled to us, and reconcile us to them, and by that means have clear consciences before God and man.—Send out Missionaries to convert the Heathens, many of whom after they cease to worship gods, which neither see nor hear, become ten times more the children of Hell, then ever they were, why what is the reason? Why the reason is obvious, they must learn to do justice at home, before they go into distant lands, to display their charity, Christianity, and benevolence; when they learn to do justice, God will accept their offering, (no man may think that I am against Missionaries for I am not, my object is to see justice done at home, before we go to convert the Heathens.)

A Nat Turner Chronology
(1800–1832)

1800 Nat Turner born on October 2 in Southampton County, Virginia, the property of Benjamin Turner II.

Gabriel Prosser conspiracy exposed in Richmond, Virginia.

1803–
1809 Turner impresses his family and community with his extraordinary intelligence and abilities.

1809 Benjamin Turner gives Nat Turner to his son Samuel.

1816 American Colonization Society founded to arrange the transportation of free blacks to Africa.

1818–
1822 Nat Turner may have married Cherry.

1822 Samuel Turner dies, and after final settlement of the estate, Nat Turner becomes the property of Thomas Moore and his wife, Sarah (Sally).

Denmark Vesey conspiracy discovered in Charleston, South Carolina. Thirty-five people are executed.

1821–
1825 Nat Turner experiences a series of visions involving direct communication from "the Spirit."

1825–
1828 Nat Turner begins to receive "the true knowledge of faith." He feels the Holy Ghost is with him, and he sees in the sky "the forms of men in different attitudes" and "the lights of the Saviour's hands."

Nat Turner baptizes himself and the white man, Etheldred Brantley.

1827 Nat Turner's owner, Thomas Moore, dies. Turner legally becomes the property of the child Putnam Moore.

1828   On May 12, the Spirit visits Turner once again and tells him "the Serpent was loosened, and Christ had laid down the yoke he had borne for the sins of men, and that I should take it on and fight against the Serpent, for the time was fast approaching when the first should be last and the last should be first."

1829   David Walker, a Boston African American, publishes the first edition of his *Appeal to the Colored Citizens of the World*, a militant attack on slavery.

1830   Sarah (Sally) Moore (Thomas Moore's widow and the mother of Turner's master, the child Putnam Moore) marries local wheelwright Joseph Travis.

1831   *January 1*   William Lloyd Garrison begins publication of the abolitionist newspaper, *The Liberator.*

February 12   Nat Turner interprets a solar eclipse as a heavenly sign to prepare for the rebellion.

July 4   Nat Turner originally plans the rebellion to begin on this day. It is postponed when he becomes ill.

August 13   The sun appears to turn bluish-green to observers all along the east coast of the United States. Turner interprets this as a final sign that he can no longer delay the rebellion.

August 21, early afternoon   The conspirators gather for a dinner at Cabin Pond. Hark, Henry, Nelson, Sam, Jack, and Will cook a pig and drink brandy. Nat Turner joins them belatedly at around 3:00 P.M.

August 22, around 2:00 A.M.   The rebellion begins with the murder of the Joseph Travis family.

August 22, early morning to end of day   The rebels move from house to house in the neighborhood (occasionally skipping some) and kill every white man, woman, and child they encounter.

August 22, later in the day   On their way to Jerusalem, the rebels stop to pick up recruits at the James W. Parker farm. They scatter and retreat after encountering militia.

Nat Turner tries to regroup with a sufficient number of rebels to attack the town of Jerusalem. He fails.

August 22–23, night   Nat Turner and a group of rebels spend the night near Major Ridley's plantation. A false alarm frightens many away.

August 23, just before daybreak   Nat Turner leads an attack on the farm of Dr. Simon Blunt. The house is defended by the residents, and several of the rebels are shot.

August 23   The remaining rebels encounter a party of whites at the Newitt Harris house and break up as an organized group.

Nat Turner conceals himself in the woods with two other rebels. Near nightfall Turner directs the two to search for other rebels and to gather them at Cabin Pond.

August 24   Nat Turner remains all day alone at Cabin Pond, waiting in vain for other rebels to join him.

August 25   Nat Turner steals supplies from the Travis residence and finds a hiding place in a hole under a pile of fence rails in a field.

Turner remains in hiding between August 25 and October 30.

August 31   The first rebels are tried at the Southampton County Court of Oyer and Terminer.

September 4   The executions begin.

October 30, near noon   Nat Turner captured by Benjamin Phipps.

October 31   Nat Turner delivered to the Southampton County jail.

November 1–3   Nat Turner interviewed in his jail cell by Thomas R. Gray.

November 5   Nat Turner tried, convicted, and sentenced to be executed.

November 10   Thomas R. Gray procures a copyright for *The Confessions of Nat Turner.*

November 11   Nat Turner is hanged.

November 25   Gray publishes *The Confessions of Nat Turner.*

1832   *January and February*   The Virginia House of Delegates debates the issue of emancipation.

January   New England Anti-Slavery Society founded in Boston.

March   The Virginia House of Delegates restricts black preaching and tightens the slave code.

September   Thomas R. Dew of William and Mary College publishes "Abolition of Negro Slavery," in *The American Quarterly Review.*

Questions for Consideration

1. Describe Nat Turner's family and the nature of his childhood. Characterize his personality and core values.
2. Describe Turner's religious beliefs and practices.
3. What motivated Turner to begin the rebellion?
4. Describe Turner's goals and tactics for the rebellion.
5. Was Nat Turner regarded as a leader by the enslaved people of Southampton County? What were the sources of his authority?
6. What did the rebellion accomplish? Do you regard it as successful or unsuccessful? By what criteria is it appropriate to judge success or failure?
7. Describe the reaction of the white population to news of the rebellion. Why did it react the way it did?
8. Who is the author of *The Confessions of Nat Turner*? How can you determine whose voice shaped the various parts of the document?
9. What do the *Confessions* tell you about Thomas R. Gray's attitude toward Nat Turner?
10. What kind of information might Nat Turner have withheld in his confession to Gray? How can you know?
11. What were the roles of black men and women in the rebellion? What were the roles of white men and women in their response to the rebellion?
12. What techniques did the white community use to repress the rebellion? What was the role of violence? What was the role of the courts?
13. According to Thomas R. Dew, why was it impractical for Virginians to adopt any plan of emancipation after the Nat Turner rebellion?
14. Discuss the major similarities and differences between Nat Turner's *Confessions* and David Walker's *Appeal*.
15. Do you regard Nat Turner as a great American leader? Why or why not?
16. Why should Americans of the twenty-first century be interested in studying the Nat Turner rebellion?

Selected Bibliography

THE NAT TURNER REBELLION

Books

Allmendinger, David F., Jr. *Nat Turner and the Rising in Southampton County*. Baltimore: Johns Hopkins University Press, 2014.

Aptheker, Herbert. *Nat Turner's Slave Rebellion*. New York: Humanities Press, 1966.

Breen, Patrick H. *The Land Shall Be Deluged in Blood: A New History of the Nat Turner Revolt*. Oxford: Oxford University Press, 2015.

Drewry, William Sidney. *The Southampton Insurrection*. Washington, D.C.: Neale Company, 1900.

French, Scot. *The Rebellious Slave: Nat Turner in American Memory*. New York: Houghton Mifflin, 2004.

Greenberg, Kenneth S., ed. *Nat Turner: A Slave Rebellion in History and Memory*. Oxford: Oxford University Press, 2003.

Harding, Vincent. *There Is a River: The Black Struggle for Freedom in America*. New York: Vintage Books, 1983.

Oates, Stephen B. *The Fires of Jubilee: Nat Turner's Fierce Rebellion*. New York: New American Library, 1975.

Parramore, Thomas C. *Southampton County, Virginia*. Charlottesville: University Press of Virginia for the Southampton County Historical Society, 1978.

Scully, Randolph Ferguson. *Religion and the Making of Nat Turner's Virginia: Baptist Community and Conflict, 1740–1840*. Charlottesville: University of Virginia Press, 2008.

Sundquist, Eric J. *To Wake the Nations: Race in the Making of American Literature*. Cambridge, Mass.: Belknap Press of Harvard University Press, 1993.

Tragle, Henry Irving, ed. *The Southampton Slave Revolt of 1831: A Compilation of Source Material*. Amherst: University of Massachusetts Press, 1971.

Films

The Birth of a Nation. Nate Parker, Director. Jean McGianni Celestin, Nate Parker, Writers. Fox Searchlight Pictures, Distributor. 2016.
Nat Turner: A Troublesome Property. Charles Burnett, Director. Charles Burnett, Frank Christopher, and Kenneth S. Greenberg, Writers. California Newsreel, Distributor. 2003.

Articles

Crofts, Daniel W. "Communities in Revolt: An Introduction." *Journal of the Early Republic* 27, no. 4 (Winter 2007): 655–60.
Elliott, Robert N. "The Nat Turner Insurrection as Reported in the North Carolina Press." *North Carolina Historical Review* 38, no. 1 (January 1961): 1–18.
Hildebrand, Reginald F. "'An Imperious Sense of Duty': Documents Illustrating an Episode in the Methodist Reaction to the Nat Turner Revolt." *Methodist History* 19 (April 1981): 155–74.
Horwitz, Tony. "Untrue Confessions: Is Most of What We Know about the Slave Rebel Nat Turner Wrong?" *New Yorker*, December 13, 1999, 80–89.
Kaye, Anthony E. "Neighborhoods and Nat Turner: The Making of a Slave Rebel and the Unmaking of a Slave Rebellion." *Journal of the Early Republic* 27, no. 4 (Winter 2007): 705–20.
Santoro, Anthony. "The Prophet in His Own Words: Nat Turner's Biblical Construction." *Virginia Magazine of History and Biography* 116, no. 2 (2008): 114–49.
Scully, Randolph Ferguson. "'I Come Here Before You Did and I Shall Not Go Away': Race, Gender, and Evangelical Community on the Eve of the Nat Turner Rebellion." *Journal of the Early Republic* 27, no. 4 (Winter 2007): 661–84.

VIRGINIA AFTERMATH OF THE NAT TURNER REBELLION

Books

Crofts, Daniel W. *Old Southampton: Politics and Society in a Virginia County, 1834–1869.* Charlottesville: University Press of Virginia, 1992.
Freehling, Alison Goodyear. *Drift toward Dissolution: The Virginia Slavery Debate of 1831–1832.* Baton Rouge: Louisiana State University Press, 1982.
Robert, Joseph C. *The Road from Monticello: A Study of the Virginia Slavery Debate of 1832.* Durham, N.C.: Duke University Press, 1941.

Articles

Breen, Patrick H. "Contested Communion: The Limits of White Solidarity in Nat Turner's Virginia." *Journal of the Early Republic* 27, no. 4 (Winter 2007): 685–703.

Stampp, Kenneth M. "An Analysis of Thomas R. Dew's 'Review of the Debates in the Virginia Legislature.'" *Journal of Negro History* 27 (October 1942): 380–87.

Tomlins, Christopher L. "In Nat Turner's Shadow: Reflections on the Norfolk Dry Dock Affair of 1830–1831." *Labor History* 33, no. 4 (Fall 1992): 494–518.

WILLIAM STYRON AND THE CONFESSIONS OF NAT TURNER

Books

Casciato, Arthur D., and James L. W. West III, eds. *Critical Essays on William Styron*. Boston: G. K. Hall, 1982.

Clarke, John Henrik, ed. *William Styron's Nat Turner: Ten Black Writers Respond*. Boston: Beacon Press, 1968.

Davis, Mary Kemp. *Nat Turner Before the Bar of Judgment: Fictional Treatments of the Southampton Slave Insurrection*. Baton Rouge: Louisiana State University Press, 1999.

Duff, John B., and Peter M. Mitchell, eds. *The Nat Turner Rebellion: The Historical Event and the Modern Controversy*. New York: Harper and Row, 1971.

Stone, Albert E. *The Return of Nat Turner: History, Literature, and Cultural Politics in Sixties America*. Athens: University of Georgia Press, 1992.

Styron, William. *The Confessions of Nat Turner*. New York: Random House, 1967.

———. *This Quiet Dust and Other Writings*. New York: Random House, 1982.

West, James L. W. III, ed. *Conversations with William Styron*. Jackson: University of Mississippi Press, 1985.

Articles

Genovese, Eugene D. "The Nat Turner Case." *New York Review of Books*, September 12, 1968, 34–37.

Gross, Seymour L., and Eileen Bender. "History, Politics and Literature: The Myth of Nat Turner." *American Quarterly* 23 (October 1971): 487–518.

Harding, Vincent, and Eugene Genovese. "An Exchange on Nat Turner." *New York Review of Books*, November 7, 1968, 35–37.

AFRICAN AMERICAN RELIGION, REBELLION, AND RESISTANCE

Books

Camp, Stephanie M. H. *Closer to Freedom: Enslaved Women and Everyday Resistance in the Plantation South*. Chapel Hill: University of North Carolina Press, 2004.

Downey, Arthur T. *The Creole Affair: The Slave Rebellion that Led the U.S. and Great Britain to the Brink of War*. Lanham, Md.: Rowman and Littlefield, 2014.

Egerton, Douglas R. *Gabriel's Rebellion: The Virginia Slave Conspiracies of 1800 and 1802*. Chapel Hill: University of North Carolina Press, 1993.

———. *He Shall Go Out Free: The Lives of Denmark Vesey*. Madison, Wis.: Madison House, 1999.

Franklin, John Hope, and Loren Schweninger. *Runaway Slaves: Rebels on the Plantation*. New York: Oxford University Press, 1999.

Frey, Sylvia R. *Water from the Rock: Black Resistance in a Revolutionary Age*. Princeton, N.J.: Princeton University Press, 1991.

Fulop, Timothy E., and Albert J. Raboteau, eds. *African-American Religion: Interpretive Essays in History and Culture*. New York: Routledge, 1997.

Harding, Vincent. *There Is a River: The Black Struggle for Freedom in America*. New York: Harcourt, Brace, 1981.

Hinks, Peter P., ed. *David Walker's Appeal to the Colored Citizens of the World*. University Park: Pennsylvania State University Press, 2000.

———. *To Awaken My Afflicted Brethren: David Walker and the Problem of Antebellum Slave Resistance*. University Park: Pennsylvania State University Press, 1997.

Hoffer, Peter Charles. *Cry Liberty: The Great Stono Slave Rebellion of 1739*. New York: Oxford University Press, 2010.

Jordan, Winthrop D. *Tumult and Silence at Second Creek: An Inquiry into a Civil War Slave Conspiracy*. Baton Rouge: Louisiana State University Press, 1993.

Kaye, Anthony E. *Joining Places: Slave Neighborhoods in the Old South*. Chapel Hill: University of North Carolina Press, 2007.

Nicholls, Michael L. *Whispers of Rebellion: Narrating Gabriel's Conspiracy*. Charlottesville: University of Virginia Press, 2012.

Pearson, Edward A., ed. *Designs against Charleston: The Trial Record of the Denmark Vesey Slave Conspiracy of 1822*. Chapel Hill: University of North Carolina Press, 1999.

Rasmussen, Daniel. *American Uprising: The Untold Story of America's Largest Slave Revolt*. New York: HarperCollins, 2011.

Rediker, Marcus. *The Amistad Rebellion: An Atlantic Odyssey of Slavery and Freedom*. New York: Viking, 2012.

Robertson, David. *Denmark Vesey: The Buried Story of America's Largest Slave Rebellion and the Man Who Led It*. New York: Vintage Books, 1999.

Rucker, Walter C. *The River Flows On: Black Resistance, Culture, and Identity Formation in Early America*. Baton Rouge: Louisiana State University Press, 2006.

Schwarz, Philip J., ed. *Gabriel's Conspiracy: A Documentary History*. Charlottesville: University of Virginia Press, 2012.

Sidbury, James. *Ploughshares into Swords: Race, Rebellion and Identity in Gabriel's Virginia, 1730–1810*. New York: Cambridge University Press, 1997.

Smith, Mark M., ed. *Stono: Documenting and Interpreting a Southern Slave Revolt*. Columbia: University of South Carolina Press, 2005.

Sundquist, Eric J. *To Wake the Nations: Race in the Making of American Literature*. Cambridge, Mass.: Belknap Press of Harvard University Press, 1993.

Index